The DESSERT BOOK

A COMPLETE MANUAL FROM THE BEST
AMERICAN AND FOREIGN AUTHORITIES

The
AMERICAN ANTIQUARIAN COOKBOOK
Collection

This facsimile edition of *The Dessert Book* by A Boston Lady was reproduced by permission from the volume in the collection of the American Antiquarian Society (AAS), Worcester, Massachusetts. Founded in 1812 by Isaiah Thomas, a Revolutionary War patriot and successful printer and publisher, the Society is a research library documenting the life of Americans from the colonial era through 1876. AAS aims to collect, preserve, and make available as complete a record as possible of the printed materials from the early American experience. The cookbook collection includes approximately 1,100 volumes.

OTHER BOOKS IN THE AMERICAN ANTIQUARIAN SOCIETY COOKBOOK COLLECTION

1776-1876: The Centennial Cook Book and General Guide, by Mrs. Ella E. Myers

American Cookery, by Amelia Simmons

The American Family Keepsake, by The Good Samaritan

The American Vine-Dresser's Guide, by John James Dufour

Apician Morsels, by Dick Humelbergius Secundus

The Appledore Cookbook, by Maria Parloa

The Art of Dining, and the Art of Attaining High Health, by Thomas Walker

Baker's Guide, by John Weild

California Recipe Book, by Ladies of California

The Canadian Housewife's Manual of Cookery

Canoe and Camp Cookery, by Seneca

The Caroline Housewife, by Sarah Rutledge

The Compleat Housewife, by Eliza Smith

The Complete Confectioner, Pastry-Cook, and Baker, by Eleanor Parkinson

The Complete Cook, by J.M. Sanderson

The Cook Book of Rare and Valuable Recipes

The Cook Not Mad

The Cook's Oracle and Housekeeper's Manual, by William Kitchiner, M.D.

The Cook's Own Book, and Housekeeper's Register, by Mrs. N.K.M. Lee

The Cooking Manual of Practical Directions for Economical Every-Day Cookery, by Juliet Corson

Cottage Economy, by William Cobbett

Confederate Receipt Book

Crumbs from the Round Table, by Joseph Barber

Dainty Dishes, by Lady Harriet E. St. Clair

Dairying Exemplified, by Josiah Twamley

De Witt's Connecticut Cook, and Housekeeper's Assistant, by Mrs. N. Orr

Directions for Cookery, by Eliza Leslie

Directions for Cooking by Troops, in Camp and Hospital, by Florence Nightingale

Domestic French Cookery, by L.E. Audot

Every Lady's Cook Book, by Mrs. T.J. Crowen

Fifteen Cent Dinners for Families of Six, by Juliet Corson

The French Cook, by Louis Eustache Ude

The Frugal Housewife, by Susannah Carter

The Frugal Housewife, by Lydia Maria Child

The Hand-Book of Carving

The Hand-Book of Practical Cookery, for Ladies and Professional Cooks, by Pierre Blot

The Health Reformer's Cook Book, by Mrs. Lucretia E. Jackson

The House Servant's Directory, by Robert Roberts

The Housekeeper's Manual

How to Mix Drinks, by Jerry Thomas

The Hygienic Cook Book, by John Harvey Kellogg

Jewish Cookery Book, by Esther Levy

The Kansas Home Cook-Book, by the Ladies of Leavenworth

Mackenzie's Five Thousand Receipts in All the Useful and Domestic Arts, by Colin Mackenzie

Miss Beecher's Domestic Receipt Book, by Catharine Beecher

Miss Leslie's New Cookery Book, by Eliza Leslie

Modern Cookery, In All Its Branches, by Eliza Acton and Sarah J. Hale

Modern Domestic Cookery, and *Useful Receipt Book*, by W. A. Henderson

The Modern Family Receipt Book, by Mrs. Mary Holland

Mrs. Hale's New Cook Book, by Mrs. Sarah J. Hale

Mrs. Owen's Illinois Cook Book, by Mrs. T.J.V. Owens

Mrs. Porter's New Southern Cookery Book, by Mrs. M.E. Porter

My Mother's Cook Book, by Ladies of St. Louis

The National Cook Book, by Eliza Leslie

New American Cookery, by An American Lady

The New Art of Cookery, by Richard Briggs

The New England Cook Book

The New England Economical Housekeeper, and Family Receipt Book, by Esther A. Howland

The New Housekeeper's Manual, by Catherine E. Beecher and Harriet Beecher Stowe

The New Hydropathic Cook Book, by Russell Thacher Trall

The New Whole Art of Confectionary, by W. Young

Nouvelle Cuisiniere Canadienne

One Thousand Valuable Secrets in the Elegant and Useful Arts

The Pantropheon, by Alexis Soyer

The People's Manual, by Perrin Bliss

The Philosophy of Eating, by Albert Bellows

The Physiology of Taste, by Jean A. Brillat-Savarin

The Picayune's Creole Cookbook, by The Picayune

The Practical Distiller, by John Wyeth

Presbyterian Cook Book

Science in the Kitchen, by Thomas Hopkins and Mrs. L.A. Hopkins

Seventy-Five Receipts for Pastry, Cakes, and Sweetmeats, by Eliza Leslie

The Times' Recipes, by The New York Times

Total Abstinence Cookery

A Treatise on Bread, by Sylvester Graham

Vegetable Diet, by William Alcott

The Virginia Housewife, by Mary Randolph

What to Do with the Cold Mutton

What to Eat and How to Cook It, by Joseph Cowan

The Young Housekeeper, by William Alcott

The DESSERT BOOK

A COMPLETE MANUAL FROM THE BEST
AMERICAN AND FOREIGN AUTHORITIES

A BOSTON LADY

**Andrews McMeel
Publishing, LLC**

Kansas City • Sydney • London

The Dessert Book copyright © 2013 by American Antiquarian Society. All rights reserved. Printed in the United States of America. No part of this book may be used or reproduced in any manner whatsoever without written permission except in the case of reprints in the context of reviews.

Andrews McMeel Publishing, LLC
an Andrews McMeel Universal company
1130 Walnut Street, Kansas City, Missouri 64106

www.andrewsmcmeel.com

ISBN: 978-1-4494-5506-4

Editor's Note: Page numbers 105-112 were omitted in the original publication. There is no material missing in this edition.

ATTENTION: SCHOOLS AND BUSINESSES
Andrews McMeel books are available at quantity discounts with bulk purchase for educational, business, or sales promotional use. For information, please e-mail the Andrews McMeel Publishing Special Sales Department: specialsales@amuniversal.com

THE
DESSERT BOOK:

A COMPLETE MANUAL

FROM THE BEST AMERICAN AND FOREIGN
AUTHORITIES.

WITH

ORIGINAL ECONOMICAL RECIPES.

BY A BOSTON LADY.

BOSTON:
J. E. TILTON AND COMPANY.
1872.

Entered, according to Act of Congress, in the year 1871,

By J. E. TILTON & CO.,

In the Office of the Librarian of Congress, at Washington.

INTRODUCTION.

WHILE the preparation of soups, joints, and gravies is left to ruder and stronger hands, the delicate fingers of the lady of the household, are best fitted to mingle the proportions of exquisite desserts. It is absolutely necessary to the economy of the household that this art should form a part of every lady's education. For these reasons we offer this book to the public. It will be found useful both by the rich and by those of more moderate means; the common mistake of giving none but expensive receipts having been carefully avoided.

Before entering upon our main subject we think it will not be out of place to offer a few remarks on that very important subject, the arrangement of dishes with an eye to proper effect. On the style and elegance in which a dessert-table is spread, much of its success depends. In arranging the table, the greater number of handsome dishes and high stands that can be available the better, as glacés fruits, compotes, and confectionery look much handsomer when so displayed than they could possibly do in low or flat dishes. Vases of natural flowers tastefully interspersed throughout the table heighten the effect, and should never be absent. It is considered out of taste to mix cake, fruits, and bonbons on the same dish or stand: each kind should be grouped in its separate receptacle, and these alternated on the table according as taste will suggest. Ices, of course, will be served moulded into pyramids or other effective forms; and there are numerous designs to be had which are highly artistic and ornamental for iced pudding, jellies, and blanc-mange, all of which will add beauty and elegance to the table. Even with the most minute directions we can give, the artiste must rely, after all, on his own taste as to the proper disposition and grouping of colors, shapes, and sizes; but a little experience will enable him to produce the finest effects, which will well repay the trouble and study it may cost.

CONTENTS.

CHAPTER I.

PUDDINGS AND PIES.

TAPIOCA CREAM. — SNOW PUDDING. — BATTER PUDDING. — SUET PUDDING. — CHOCOLATE MERINGUE. — CRACKER PUDDING. — CABINET PUDDING. — BREAD PUDDING. — RICE MERINGUE. — OMELET SOUFFLE. — WINE JELLY MERINGUE. — INDIAN PUDDING. — SPURGE PUDDING. — SPANISH CREAM. — QUEEN OF PUDDINGS. — CHOCOLATE CREAM PIE. — LEMON PIE. — MARLBOROUGH PIE. — CORN STARCH PIE. — CREAM PIE. — MERINGUE PIE. — MINCE PIE. 13

CHAPTER II.

CAKE-MAKING.

ICING CAKES. — TO ICE AND ORNAMENT A WEDDING-CAKE. — POUND CAKES. — PLUM-CAKE OR WEDDING-CAKE. — ORANGE BISCUITS. — MACAROONS. — MACAROONS SOUFFLÉS. — ITALIAN MACAROONS. — RATAFIAS. — SWEDISH MACAROONS. — STICKS OF VANILLA. — STICKS OF CINNAMON. — GENOESE PASTE 19

CHAPTER III.

MASSEPAINS AND ALMOND-CAKES IN GENERAL.

MASSEPAINS PLAIN.—MASSEPAINS SOUFFLÉS.—ORNAMENTAL ROUT-CAKES. —FILBERTS, FAGOTS, CARROTS, TURNIPS, WALNUTS, BALLS, HEARTS, RINGS, TREFOIL. — ALMOND CROCKETS, VARIOUS. — ALMOND CRACKLINGS, VARIOUS. — PISTACHIO MACAROONS. — FILBERT MACAROONS.— BRUSSELS MACAROONS. — MOIST MACAROONS.— DUTCH MACAROONS.— SPANISH MACAROONS. — VICTORIA MACAROONS. — CHOCOLATE MACAROONS 26

CHAPTER IV.

ALMOND SOUFFLÉ ROUT-CAKES.

FRASCATI CROQUANTES. — SMALL SOUFFLÉS IN CASES. — SMALL SOUFFLÉS OF PISTACHIOS.— SMALL SOUFFLÉS WITH CHOCOLATE.— DIAVOLINI.— SMALL SOUFFLÉS WITH CANDIED PEELS.— ZEPHYR SOUFFLÉS.— ZEPHYR SOUFFLÉS WITH PISTACHIOS. — ZEPHYR SOUFFLÉS, ROSE PINK. — ALMOND SOUFFLÉS. — PISTACHIO SOUFFLÉS 35

CHAPTER V

CAKES, JUMBLES, &c.

SPONGE-CAKE. — CUP-CAKE. — QUEEN-CAKE.— JUMBLES. —JELLY-CAKE. — KISSES. — COCOANUT-CAKE. — LADY-CAKE. — CHARLOTTE RUSSE, 40

CHAPTER VI.

DESSERT WAFERS IN GENERAL.

ITALIAN WAFERS. — FRENCH WAFERS. — FLEMISH GAUFFRES. — FRENCH GAUFFRES. — SPANISH WAFERS. — GINGER WAFERS 43

CHAPTER VII.

LONG BISCUITS ICED, AND DIFFERENT SORTS OF MERINGUES.

GENERAL REMARKS ON MERINGUES. — ORDINARY MERINGUES. — CREAM-ICED MERINGUES. — MERINGUES WITH PRESERVE. — ITALIAN MERINGUES. — ITALIAN MERINGUES GARNISHED. — ICED ITALIAN MERINGUES.

Contents. 7

— MERINGUES IN THE FORM OF CAULIFLOWERS. — MERINGUES IN THE FORM OF MUSHROOMS. — MERINGUES IN THE FORM OF STRAWBERRIES. — MERINGUES IN THE FORM OF GRAPES. — LONG OBTUSE-POINTED BISCUITS ICED WITH CHOCOLATE. — LONG OBTUSE-POINTED BISCUITS WITH ROSE-PINK ICING. — LONG OBTUSE-POINTED BISCUITS WITH WHITE ICING. — LONG OBTUSE-POINTED BISCUITS WITH SPINACH-GREEN ICING. — LONG OBTUSE-POINTED BISCUITS WITH COFFEE ICING   47

CHAPTER VIII

DIFFERENT KINDS OF NOUGAT, PASTAFROLLE, AND CHESTNUT BISCUITS.

ORDINARY NOUGAT. — PARISIAN NOUGATS. — NOUGAT DE MARSEILLES. — TORONI BIANCA. — TORONI ROSSA. — TORONI WITH PISTACHIOS. — PASTAFROLLE. — NEAPOLITAN GLACÉS, WHITE. — NEAPOLITAN CAKE. — NEAPOLITAN GLACÉS WITH CHOCOLATE. — BONBON TARTLETS, ROSE-PINK. — BONBON TARTLETS, WHITE. — BONBON TARTLETS WITH CHOCOLATE. — BONBON TARTLETS OF GREENGAGE. — BONBON TARTLETS OF APRICOT. — BONBON ALMOND-PASTE ROUT-CAKES -   55

CHAPTER IX.

BOUCHÉES, OR DESSERT-CAKES, GLACÉS WITH WHOLE FRUITS AND PRESERVES.

GENERAL REMARKS. — BOUCHÉES DE DAMES. — BOUCHÉES WITH APRICOTS. — BOUCHÉES WITH GREEN APRICOTS. — BOUCHÉES WITH PINE-APPLE. — BOUCHÉES WITH CHERRIES. — BOUCHÉES WITH GREENGAGES. — BOUCHÉES WITH PEACHES. — BOUCHÉES WITH ORANGES. — BOUCHÉES GARNISHED WITH PRESERVE   61

CHAPTER X.

ICE CREAMS.

GENERAL DIRECTIONS. — LEMON OR VANILLA ICE CREAM. — CHOCOLATE CREAM ICE. — FLOWING ICED PUNCH. — MARASCHINO ICE CREAM. — PINE-APPLE CREAM ICE. — ORANGE CREAM ICE. — GINGER CREAM ICE. — ITALIAN CREAM ICE. — PISTACHIO CREAM ICE. — ORANGE-FLOWER CREAM ICE. — NOUGAT CREAM ICE. — LIQUEUR CREAM ICE. — BOURBON CREAM ICE. — CHESTERFIELD CREAM ICE. — WHOLE-RICE CREAM ICE. — STRAWBERRY CREAM ICE. — RASPBERRY CREAM ICE. — APRICOT CREAM ICE. — PEACH CREAM ICE. — CHERRY CREAM ICE   64

Contents.

CHAPTER XI.

WATER AND FRUIT ICES.

FRUIT WATER ICE. — RED-CURRANT WATER ICE. — RASPBERRY WATER ICE. — STRAWBERRY WATER ICE. — CHERRY WATER ICE. — PINE-APPLE WATER ICE. — ORANGE WATER ICE. — LEMON WATER ICE. — PEACH WATER ICE. — APRICOT WATER ICE. — GREENGAGE WATER ICE. — DAMSON WATER ICE. — POMEGRANATE WATER ICE. — BARBERRY WATER ICE. — TUTTIFRUTTI, OR MACEDOINE WATER ICE   73

CHAPTER XII.

IMITATION SOUFFLÉS ICED, AND BISCUITS ICED.

IMITATION SOUFFLÉ ICED À LA LONDONDERRY. — SOUFFLÉ ICED À LA WALTER SCOTT. — SOUFFLÉ ICED À LA BYRON. — SOUFFLÉ ICED À LA CHARLES KEAN. — ICED BISCUITS À LA CHARLES DICKENS. — ICED BISCUITS À LA THACKERAY   78

CHAPTER XIII.

ICED PUDDINGS.

ICED PUDDING À LA PERCY BYSSHE SHELLEY. — ICED PUDDING À LA SHAKSPEARE. — ICED PUDDING À LA VICTORIA. — ICED PUDDING À LA KEMBLE   82

CHAPTER XIV.

ICED BEVERAGES CALLED GRANITI.

GENERAL INSTRUCTIONS. — ORGEAT, OR MILK OF ALMONDS. — COFFEE GRANITO. — ANOTHER METHOD OF FREEZING GRANITI. — CLARET GRANITO. — SHERRY GRANITO. — PUNCH GRANITO. — FRUIT-JUICE GRANITO   84

CHAPTER XV

DIFFERENT KINDS OF ICED PUNCH.

GIN PUNCH. — RUM PUNCH. — REGENT PUNCH. — BISHOP. — HEIDELBERG BISHOP. — PRINCE-OF-WALES PUNCH. — CHESTERFIELD PUNCH. — BEAUFORT PUNCH. — ROMAN PUNCH. — ROMAN PUNCH À LA MONTROSE.   86

CHAPTER XVI.

COFFEE.

HISTORY OF THE PLANT. — QUALITIES OF COFFEE. — MOCHA. — CAYENNE COFFEE. — BOURBON COFFEE. — MARTINIQUE COFFEE. — ST. DOMINGO COFFEE. — JAVA COFFEE. — CEYLON COFFEE. — ON ROASTING COFFEE. — COFFEE AS A BEVERAGE   89

CHAPTER XVII.

CHOCOLATE.

THE CACAO-TREE. — VARIETIES OF CACAO. — BUTTER OF CACAO. — CHOCOLATE AS A BEVERAGE. — WHAT CHOCOLATE SHOULD BE. — PREPARATION OF CHOCOLATE. — COMMON CHOCOLATE, NO. 1. — CHOCOLATE DE SANTÉ, NOS. 2, 3, 4, AND 5. — CHOCOLATE, NOS. 6, 7, 8, AND 9. — CHOCOLATE WITHOUT SUGAR. — LADIES' CHOCOLATE. — MARBLED CHOCOLATE. — BAYONNE OR SPANISH CHOCOLATE. — TONIC SALEP CHOCOLATE. — TONIC TAPIOCA CHOCOLATE. — TONIC SAGO CHOCOLATE. — ARROWROOT CHOCOLATE. — WHITE CHOCOLATES. — MANNER OF PREPARING THE BEVERAGE. — WATER CHOCOLATE. — MILK CHOCOLATE. — GERMAN MILK CHOCOLATE. — CREAM CHOCOLATE. — ALMOND MILK CHOCOLATE. — COMMON EGG CHOCOLATE. — GERMAN EGG CHOCOLATE. — PARISIAN EGG CHOCOLATE. — WINE CHOCOLATE. — HASTY CHOCOLATE   107

CHAPTER XVIII.

TEA.

HISTORY OF THE PLANT. — ITS CULTIVATION. — PROPERTIES OF TEA. — ADULTERATIONS AND PREPARATIONS. — VARIETIES OF GREEN TEA. — HYSON. — OOLONG. — PEARL GUNPOWDER. — GUNPOWDER. — IMPERIAL SOUMLO. — BLACK TEAS. — BOHEA. — PEKOE. — CONGOU. — SOUCHONG. — FICHI. — TEA: WHAT TO DRINK, AND WHEN TO DRINK IT. — LADY-APPLE TEA. — TEA LIQUEUR. — ENGLISH TEA. — POLISH TEA. — ROSE-LEAF TEA   125

CHAPTER XIX.

LEMONADES AND ACIDULATED DRINKS.

Hot Lemonade. — Milk Lemonade. — Wine Lemonade. — Tartaric Lemonade. — Citric Lemonade. — Portable Lemonade in Cakes. — Portable Lemonade in Powder. — Laville's and Fontenelle's Gaseous Lemonades. — Orangeade. — Acidulated Drinks. — Cherry Water. — Strawberry Water. — Raspberry Water. — Currant Water. — Raspberry Vinegar. — Strawberry Vinegar. — Currant Shrub - 135

CHAPTER XX.

LIQUEURS OR CORDIALS, AND SPIRITUOUS WATERS.

General Remarks. — Ratafias. — Anise-Seed Ratafia. — Angelica Ratafia. — Black-Currant Ratafia. — Absinthe or Wormwood Ratafia. — Orange-Flower Ratafia. — Raspberry Ratafia. — Ratafia of Red Fruits. — Juniper-Berry Ratafia. — Pomegranate Ratafia. — Grenoble Ratafia. — Pink Ratafia. — Neuilly Ratafia. — Seed Ratafia. — Usquebaugh. — Spirituous Waters. — General Description. — Compound Anise-Seed Water. — Andaye Brandy. — Aromatic Water. — Bergamot Water. — Cinnamon Water. — Caraway Water. — Eau Divine. — Clove Water. — Water of Pinks. — Malta Water. — Mint Water. — Almond Water. — Rosemary Water. — Tea Water. — Fine Orange Water 140

CHAPTER XXI.

SPIRITUOUS CREAMS, ELIXIRS, MISCELLANEOUS LIQUEURS, AND DOMESTIC WINES.

What Creams are. — Absinthe Cream. — Barbadoes Cream. — Cocoa Cream. — Fruit Cream. — Orange-Flower Cream with Milk and Champagne. — Jasmine Cream. — Cherry-Water Cream. — Laurel Cream. — Mint Cream. — Myrtle Cream. — Mocha Cream. — Cream of Roses. — Vanilla Cream. — Chocolate Cream. — Elixirs. — Juniper-Berry Elixir. — Elixir of Garus. — Troubadour's Elixir. — Tabouret Elixir. — Elixir of Violets. — Miscellaneous Liqueurs. — Anisettes. — Anisettes de Bourdeaux. — Balm of Mankind. — Citronelle. — Curaçoa. — Old Men's Milk. — Nectar. — Usquebaugh. — Perfect Love. — Persicot. — Domestic Wines. — Currant Wine. — Blackberry Wine. — Gooseberry Wine. — Elderberry Wine. — Strawberry Wine. — Raspberry Wine. — Rhubarb Wine 151

Contents. 11

CHAPTER XXII.

JELLIES, MARMALADES, PRESERVES.

GELATINE. — CALVES'-FOOT JELLY. — CALVES'-FOOT JELLY FROM PREPARED GELATINE — BLANCMANGE. — QUINCE JELLY. — CURRANT JELLY. — CURRANT AND RASPBERRY JELLY. — RASPBERRY JELLY. — GRAPE JELLY. — STRAWBERRY AND BLACKBERRY JELLIES. — APPLE JELLY. — CHERRY JELLY. — ORANGE-PASTE. — APRICOT JELLY. — QUINCE BREAD. — QUINCE SALMON. — QUINCE-PASTE. — APPLE-PULP. — QUINCE-JUICE. — QUINCE SNOW. — SWEET ORANGE JELLY. — DRIED ORANGE-PEEL. — LEMON JELLY. — STRAWBERRY-PASTE. — JELLY WITH SALEP. — RED OR BLACK CURRANT PASTE. — TO PRESERVE CURRANT-JUICE   161

CHAPTER XXIII.

BRANDY FRUITS.

PREPARATION OF BRANDY FRUITS. — PEACHES IN BRANDY. — APRICOTS IN BRANDY. — GREENGAGES IN BRANDY. — PLUMS IN BRANDY. — PEARS IN BRANDY. — CHERRIES IN BRANDY. — BELGIAN MODE OF BRANDYING CHERRIES. — BRANDY ORANGES. — BRANDY GRAPES. — BRANDY PEARS (ANOTHER RULE). — BRANDY QUINCES. — BRANDY MELON RINDS. — CHINESE BRANDY FRUITS   169

CHAPTER XXIV

MARMALADES OR JAMS. — CONSERVES.

WHAT MARMALADES ARE. — PEACH OR APRICOT MARMALADES. — CHERRY JAM. — MARMALADE OF ORANGE AND LEMON PEEL. — GREENGAGE MARMALADE. — ORANGE MARMALADE. — PINE-APPLE MARMALADE. — STRAWBERRY OR RASPBERRY JAM. — QUINCE MARMALADE. — PEAR MARMALADE. — FRUIT CONSERVES. — WORMWOOD CONSERVES. — ORANGE-FLOWER AND ROSE CONSERVES. — VIOLET CONSERVE. — JELLY OF FRUIT-JUICE -   176

CHAPTER XXV

COMPOTES.

APPLE COMPOTES. — COMPOTE OF WHOLE APPLES. — STUFFED APPLE COMPOTE. — COMPOTE OF APPLES GRILLÉS. — COMPOTE OF APPLE-PASTE. — COMPOTE OF APPLES À LA DUCHESSE. — COMPOTE OF APPLE JELLY. — COMPOTE OF APPLES À LA CINTRA. — COMPOTE OF APPLE MARMALADE. — COMPOTE OF PEARS, WHITE. — COMPOTE OF

PEARS, PINK. — COMPOTE OF PEARS À LA PRINCESSE. — COMPOTE OF PEARS À LA VICTORIA. — COMPOTE OF PEARS, VARIEGATED. — COMPOTE OF PEARS À LA ZINGARA. — COMPOTE OF ORANGES. — COMPOTE OF ORANGES À L'ESPAGNOLE. — APRICOT COMPOTE. — CHESTNUT COMPOTE. — CHESTNUT COMPOTE WITH CREAM. — STRAWBERRY COMPOTE. — GREEN GOOSEBERRY COMPOTE. — CHERRY COMPOTE. — PEACH COMPOTE. — ANOTHER PEAR COMPOTE. — COMPOTE OF ROAST PEARS. — GRAPE COMPOTE. — SALADE D'ORANGES. — COMPOTE OF ORANGE BASKETS FILLED WITH FRUITS. — COMPOTE OF LEMON BASKETS. — COMPOTE OF CHERRIES. — COMPOTE OF CURRANTS. — COMPOTE OF CURRANTS IN BUNCHES. — COMPOTE OF PLUMS. — COMPOTE OF APRICOTS. — COMPOTE OF GREENGAGES. — COMPOTE OF POMEGRANATES. — COMPOTE OF ARLEQUINADE. — COMPOTE OF GREEN FIGS. — ANOTHER COMPOTE OF PEACHES. — COMPOTE OF PEACHES GRILLÉS. — ANOTHER COMPOTE OF PINE-APPLE. — COMPOTE OF WHOLE ORANGES. — COMPOTE OF WHOLE LEMONS. — COMPOTE OF IMITATION GINGER. — COMPOTE OF CHESTNUTS GLACÉS. — COMPOTE OF CHESTNUT PASTE. — COMPOTE OF VERMACELLIED CHESTNUTS. — COMPOTE OF GREEN WALNUTS. — COMPOTE OF GREEN FILBERTS. — COMPOTE OF BARBERRIES. — COMPOTE OF CRAB-APPLES. — COMPOTE OF CRANBERRIES. — COMPOTE OF GRAPES. — COMPOTE OF DRIED NORMANDY PIPPINS. — COMPOTE OF COCOANUT, WHITE. — COMPOTE OF COCOANUT, PINK. — COMPOTE OF DRIED FRUITS IN APPLE JELLY. — COMPOTE OF SPANISH BRANCO. — COMPOTE OF SANDWICHES À LA SEVILLANE. — COMPOTE À LA XIMENES. — COMPOTE OF SPANISH VERMICELLI. — PRUNE COMPOTE. — PINE-APPLE COMPOTE. — DIPLOMATIC APPLE COMPOTE. — PORTUGUESE COMPOTE. — DIVERSIFIED COMPOTE 180

THE DESSERT BOOK.

CHAPTER I.

PUDDINGS AND PIES.

TAPIOCA CREAM. — SNOW PUDDING. — BATTER PUDDING. — SUET PUDDING. — CHOCOLATE MERINGUE. — CRACKER PUDDING. — CABINET PUDDING. — BREAD PUDDING. — RICE MERINGUE. — OMELET SOUFFLE. — WINE JELLY MERINGUE. — INDIAN PUDDING. — SPURGE PUDDING. — SPANISH CREAM. — QUEEN OF PUDDINGS. — CHOCOLATE CREAM PIE. — LEMON PIE. — MARLBOROUGH PIE. — CORN STARCH PIE. — CREAM PIE. — MERINGUE PIE. — MINCE PIE.

TAPIOCA CREAM.

Soak 2 tablespoonfuls of tapioca over night, in cold water enough to cover it. 1 quart of milk to boiling point, then stir in the tapioca, and let that boil up. Add the yolks of 3 well-beaten eggs. A little salt. 1 cup of sugar. Let it all boil up, then put in the dish it is to be served in. Flavor with lemon. Beat the whites to a stiff froth, and stir in lightly. An extra one may be added just before being served. To be eaten cold.

SNOW PUDDING.

Pour 1 pint boiling water on ½ box of gelatine, stir until all is dissolved. When nearly cold strain it, and add the whites of 3 eggs, well-beaten, with 2 cups of sugar and the juice of 1 lemon. It is well to beat it, as the Charlotte Russe is done.

Take the yolks with 1 pint of milk, 1 teaspoonful corn starch, 1 extra egg, 3 small tablespoonfuls of sugar, and make a boiled custard, to be poured over the pudding when served. Flavor with wine.

BATTER PUDDING.

8 great spoonfuls flour, 1 quart milk, 4 or 8 eggs, little salt. Bake in cups or boil.

SUET PUDDING.

3 coffee cups of flour, 1 do. do. of finely-chopped suet, 1 do. do. of milk, ⅔ do. do. molasses, 1 do. do. of chopped raisins, 1 teaspoonful of saleratus, 1 teaspoonful of cloves, 1 small nutmeg. A little salt.

First mix 2 cups of the flour with the suet, then add milk and other ingredients, and the other cup of flour. Boil 3 or 4 hours.

CHOCOLATE MERINGUE.

1 quart of milk, 5 eggs, 1 square of chocolate, 3 tablespoonfuls of sugar, 1 teaspoonful corn starch.

Scrape the chocolate into the milk, and boil with the sugar. Then stir in the yolks of the eggs, with the corn starch, mixed smooth with a little milk. Boil until it begins to thicken, then pour into a pudding dish, and when a little cool, spread over the whites of the eggs beaten to a stiff froth with two thirds of a cup of sugar. Brown in oven.

VERY NICE CRACKER PUDDING.

3 large crackers to 1 quart milk, 3 eggs, 1 large spoonful sugar, a little salt, small piece of butter, very little rose-water, raisins, very little peach-water, lemon, nutmeg, brandy and wine to taste.

CABINET PUDDING.

1 cup of molasses, 1 cup of sweet milk, 1 cup of currants, ½ cup of finely-chopped suet, 1 teapoonsful soda, 1 teaspoonful cream tartar, ½ teaspoonful salt, 3 or 4 cups of flour, very little nutmeg.

All should be very thoroughly mixed together and turned into a thin pudding mould, well buttered, and boiled three or four hours. To be eaten hot with wine sauce.

BREAD PUDDING.

1 ten-cent loaf bread to 2 quarts milk, 3 eggs, ½ cup molasses, a little sugar, little salt, 2 spoonfuls cinnamon, little nutmeg, little butter, 1 spoonful cloves, ½ spoonful allspice, 1 lb. raisins. Bake slow three or four hours.

RICE MERINGUE.

1 cup of rice well boiled. 1 pint of milk, yolks of 5 eggs, rind of 1 large lemon. Bake.

Beat the whites with one pint sugar and the lemon juice, spread over the top, and brown.

OMELET SOUFFLE.

Beat the yolks of 8 eggs with 7 tablespoonfuls of sugar, the rind of 1 lemon and the juice.

Beat the whites to a stiff froth, then stir lightly together. Put in a buttered dish, and bake fifteen minutes. It must be sent to the table immediately, for if it stands a minute it will fall.

WINE JELLY MERINGUE.

Fill a dish about ⅔ full with wine jelly. Take the whites of 6 or 8 eggs beat to a stiff froth with 3 tablespoonfuls of sugar, and spread over the top of the jelly. Make a boiled custard with the yolks flavored with wine, and put a little over the jelly when served.

Take some thin slices of sponge cake dry, dip in wine, and place a thin layer in a pudding dish, pour over a little boiled custard (made with the yolks of eggs), another layer of cake, &c.

Beat the white to a stiff froth, with half a cup of sugar; spread over the top, and brown in the oven, to be eaten cold.

INDIAN PUDDING.

7 tablespoonfuls of Indian meal, 1 cup of molasses, 1 teaspoonful salt, 1 quart of milk. Boil half the milk, pour it on the meal, and let it boil up. Add molasses and salt. When cold, add the rest of the milk, and bake in a slow oven three or four hours. It is much nicer to add more milk or water without stirring while baking.

SPONGE PUDDING.

3 eggs, their weight in sugar, butter, and flour, 1 teaspoonful of cream tartar, $\frac{1}{2}$ teaspoonful of soda dissolved in a little extract of lemon. To be eaten with wine sauce.

SPANISH CREAM.

$\frac{1}{2}$ box gelatine, soak one hour in $\frac{1}{2}$ pint of milk. Beat the whites of 6 eggs to a stiff froth in a *deep dish*. Put in a cool place till ready to use. Put 1 quart of milk on to boil; beat the yolks of the eggs with sugar to taste, and when the milk is just ready to boil stir into it the yolks and the gelatine. Let it thicken as for a custard, and pour it boiling hot over the whites of the eggs, stirring all the time. Flavor with vanilla to taste.

Put in moulds, and let it stand at least four hours before using. In warm weather make it the day before.

QUEEN OF PUDDINGS.

1 pint fine bread crumbs; yolks of 4 eggs, well beaten; grated rind of 1 lemon, piece of butter the size of an egg. Bake until done, taking care not to have it watery. Whip

the whites of the eggs, and beat in a tea-cup of sugar with the lemon juice.

Spread over the pudding a layer of sweetmeats or jelly. Put the whites of the eggs over, and brown in the oven; to be eaten cold with cream.

CHOCOLATE CREAM PIE.

½ lb. sweet vanilla chocolate grated, 1 coffee-cup powdered sugar, yolks of 2 eggs, 1 gill boiling milk. Stir all together until it makes a cream.

To be spread between some very nice cake.

LEMON PIE.

3 cups of sugar, 6 eggs, 12 tablespoonfuls of water, 3 lemons and the rind grated. Beat the sugar and eggs to a foam. Add the juice of lemon then the water.

This will make two large pies.

MARLBOROUGH PIE.

1 quart of strained apple-sauce, 4 eggs, rind of 3 lemons grated, 2 cups of sugar or more, a piece of butter the size of an egg. Bake thin, with no top crust.

CORN STARCH PIE.

3 tablespoonfuls of corn starch, 1 quart of milk, yolks of 3 eggs, 3 tablespoonfuls of sugar. Flavor to taste. To be boiled as custard. Put in deep plates and bake.

Take the whites of the eggs and beat to a stiff froth, with three tablespoonfuls of sugar, spread on the top and brown.

CREAM PIE.

Beat 3 eggs 2 minutes, add 1½ cups of sifted sugar, beat 5 minutes; 1 cup of flour with 1 teaspoonful of cream tartar, beat 1 minute; ½ teaspoonful of soda in ½ tea-cup of water; add another cup of flour. A little lemon juice, and the rind grated. Bake on thin round tin plates.

CREAM FOR THE ABOVE.

Boil 1 pint of milk, beat 2 eggs with 1 coffee-cup of sugar; moisten one cup of flour and add it to the eggs. Stir this into the milk till it thickens. Flavor with lemon.

MERINGUE PIE.

The yolks of 6 eggs, juice of 2 lemons, not quite 1 cup of sugar, 1 cup of water, 2 tablespoonfuls of corn starch; to be baked on flat pie plates. After it is baked, spread the whites of 6 eggs, beat to a stiff froth, with 8 tablespoonfuls of sugar, over the top; place it in the oven again and let it brown.

MINCE PIE.

10 lbs. of meat before it is boiled makes 4 lbs. after; to the 4 lbs. allow 8 lbs. apples, 2 lbs. suet after it is boiled, 2 lbs. raisins, 2 tablespoonfuls of cinnamon, 2 do. do. of cloves, 2 do. do. of essence of lemon, 1 do. do. of allspice, 4 nutmegs, rind and juice of 2 lemons, 1 pint of brandy, 1 gill of wine, 1 pint molasses, 2 quarts or more cider, 4 lbs. or more sugar, 1 cup of salt. Chop your suet and apple together.

Mix all together well, and stand over night; and if too dry, or not highly flavored enough, add more sugar, salt, brandy, or cider.

CHAPTER II.

CAKE-MAKING.

ICING CAKES. — TO ICE AND ORNAMENT A WEDDING-CAKE. — POUND CAKES. — PLUM-CAKE OR WEDDING-CAKE. — ORANGE BISCUITS. — MACAROONS. — MACAROONS SOUFFLÉS. — ITALIAN MACAROONS. — RATAFIAS. — SWEDISH MACAROONS. — STICKS OF VANILLA. — STICKS OF CINNAMON. — GENOESE PASTE.

WE come now to that important branch of the confectioner's art, — the mixing and baking of cakes; confining our attention to those known as "fine or fancy cakes." In this department, care is required that all materials, such as eggs, butter, milk, &c., should be of the best quality, fresh, and sweet: stale eggs will spoil the best cake, as will also rancid butter. Currants should be picked over, washed, and dried before using. A large bowl is the best for mixing and beating cake, and for beating butter and sugar to a cream, as is required for rich cakes, pound-cakes, &c.: the hand is the best instrument, although a wooden spoon will be found useful for stirring in other ingredients. The oven should be ready to bake the cake immediately after it is well mixed, as standing always makes cake batter heavy. A thick paper spread over the top of a cake after it begins to bake will prevent its browning too much. A large cake requires more time to bake than a loaf of bread of the same size: about an hour and a half or two hours will be sufficient to bake a pound-cake. When you think it is done, take a stiff broom-splint, and run it into the centre of the cake: if it comes out clean and dry, the cake is done. Cake is better when allowed to cool in the pan in which it is baked, as it is apt to become heavy if turned out while hot.

ICING FOR CAKES.

Put the whites of two eggs on to a pound of pulverized white sugar with a little rose or orange-flower water, and beat them together until very light. Have ready in another cup or bowl a little lemon-juice, and begin to lay on the icing in a thin coat, over the cake, with a knife, occasionally dipping it into the lemon-juice, which will enable you to smooth it nicely. When it is covered with the coat, set it in a warm place to harden, when it will be ready for the next coat, which will be much smoother and whiter than the first. When ornamental icing is required, proceed as directed below.

TO ICE AND ORNAMENT A WEDDING-CAKE.

When the plum-cake is cold, and cleared of the paper, and trimmed, place it on a baking-sheet, and cover the top with a coating of orgeat paste, one inch and a half in thickness, and dry this in the screen for an hour; then cover the whole surface of the cake with a coating of royal icing, about half an inch in thickness, and, when this has become hard, decorate it with royal icing piped on the top and sides, in tasteful ornamental designs; using also some buds and flowers, and wreaths of artificial orange-flower blossoms, to be intermixed with the other mode of decoration. The whole of the ornamentation of a wedding-cake must be white, with the exception of a wreath of blush roses.

POUND-CAKE.

Wash the salt from one pound of butter, and beat it with one pound of nice sugar till it is like cream; have one pound of flour sifted, and beat ten eggs, the whites and yolks separately; put alternately into the butter and sugar the flour and eggs; continue beating until they are all in, and the batter looks light. Now add a grated nutmeg, half a wineglassful of brandy, and some rose-water or essence of lemon; continue to beat it well until the pan is buttered and the oven ready. This will make a four-pound cake.

ANOTHER POUND-CAKE.

Ingredients: 1 lb. of flour, 1 lb. of sifted sugar, 1 lb. of butter, 8 eggs, a wineglassful of brandy, and the rind of two oranges or lemons rubbed on sugar.

Place the butter in a basin, and work it with a wooden spoon until it assumes the appearance of thick cream, then add the flour and the sugar, and the eggs gradually: when the whole is thoroughly incorporated, add the brandy, mix well together, and bake the paste, either in tin hoops, or else on baking-sheets previously greased with butter, or, in preference to this, line either the hoops or the baking-sheets with buttered paper to prevent the cake from acquiring too much color.

Dried cherries, currants, pistachios, or candied peel, may be added.

PLUM-CAKE OR WEDDING-CAKE.

Ingredients: 2½ lbs. of flour; 1½ lb. of sifted sugar; 1½ lb. of butter; 1 lb. of chopped dried cherries; 1 lb. of cleaned currants; 1½ lb. of shred orange, lemon, and green citron peels; 12 eggs; half a pint of brandy; half a gill of caramel, or burnt sugar coloring; 1 oz. of salt; 8 oz. of ground almonds; the zest of 4 oranges; 1 oz. of pounded cinnamon, cloves, nutmegs, and coriander-seeds, — all in equal proportions.

First work the butter in a large white pan with a wooden spoon until it presents the appearance of a creamy substance; next add by degrees the sugar, flour, salt, and the eggs, still continuing to work the batter the whole of the time; then add the remainder of the ingredients; and, as soon as all is thoroughly incorporated, let the preparation be poured into a proper sized tin hoop previously lined with double bands of buttered paper, and ready placed upon a stout baking-sheet, the bottom of which must be also lined with double sheets of paper. Bake in moderate heat, and be careful not to increase the heat of the oven while baking. A cake of this weight will require about two and a half hours' baking.

ORANGE BISCUITS.

Prepare the paste as directed in the foregoing, omitting the caraway-seeds, and adding, in their stead, the zest of four oranges rubbed on sugar, and scraped off; push the batter into small, round, deep moulds previously buttered, sprinkle some small shreds of candied orange-peel on their tops, dredge them over with sugar, and bake them in a very moderate heat of a light color.

MACAROONS.

Ingredients: 1 lb. of scalded sweet almonds, 1 oz. of bitter almonds, 2 lbs. of sifted sugar, about 6 whites of eggs.

When the almonds have been scalded, freed from their hulls, washed, wiped, and dried in the screen, they must be allowed to become quite cold before they are placed in the mortar; let them be thoroughly pounded into a smooth pulp, adding a little of the sugar and some of the whites of eggs occasionally, to prevent the almonds from turning oily; and, as soon as you find that the almonds are well pulverized, add by degrees the remainder of the sugar and whites of eggs, remembering that the paste must be kept quite firm. The paste being ready, cover some baking-sheets with wafer-paper, and lay out the macaroons in the form of small round balls about the size of very small walnuts; take care to place them at least an inch apart from each other; and, when the sheet is full, pass a wet paste-brush over their surfaces, push in the oven, very moderate heat, and bake them of a light fawn-color. When done, and cold, break away any excess of wafer that may cling to the edges of the macaroons, and keep them for use in a dry place.

MACAROONS SOUFFLÉS.

Prepare the paste as directed in the foregoing case, keeping it somewhat firmer; add two whites of eggs of royal icing, work both together until thoroughly incorporated, use this to fill a biscuit-forcer, and push out the macaroons upon wafer-paper, as shown in the preceding.

Bear in mind that macaroons must be baked in *very* moderate heat; otherwise, if the heat of your oven should be at all excessive, it would cause the macaroons to run into each other, and thus produce a useless mass.

The reason macaroons *soufflés* are so liable to spread is owing to the addition of the royal icing.

NOTE. — Macaroons *soufflés* may also be baked in very small plaited paper cases.

ITALIAN MACAROONS.

Prepare the macaroon paste as in the preceding, roll it out in small round balls in your hands, and, as each of these is finished, dip the whole of its surface in white nonpareils, or, as they are familiarly termed, white harlequin's eggs, and place the macaroons in rows, at distances from each other upon wafer-paper laid out on a baking-sheet: bake in moderate heat. The nonpareils must not lose their whiteness.

RATAFIAS.

Ingredients: 8 oz. of sweet almonds, 4 oz. of bitter almonds, $1\frac{1}{2}$ lb. of fine sugar, 4 whites of eggs.

Scald, skin, wash, and wipe the almonds, and, after they have been dried in the screen, pound them thoroughly, adding the whites of eggs gradually; and then work in the sugar: this will form a firm paste. Fill a macaroon or biscuit forcer with some of the paste, push it out in very small balls, cutting them off to the proper size, and allowing them to drop in rows at distances upon the wafer-paper ready placed upon baking-sheets to receive them; pass the tip of your finger moistened with water upon their surfaces, push in the oven, at *very* slack heat, and bake the ratafias of a very light color.

SWEDISH MACAROONS.

Ingredients: 12 oz. of shred almonds, 4 oz. of ground almonds, 4 oz. Indian-corn flour, 1 lb. of fine sugar, two whole eggs, the zest or rind of two oranges rubbed on sugar.

Mix the whole of these ingredients in a basin until thoroughly incorporated; then roll out the paste or mixture in balls the size of a small walnut; place these upon sheet wafer laid out on baking-sheets, push in the oven, moderate heat, and bake the swedes of a light color.

SWEDISH MACAROONS, ANOTHER WAY.

Prepare the paste as directed in the foregoing; spread it out a quarter of an inch thick on sheet wafer laid out on baking-sheets, push in the oven, moderate heat, bake of a light color; and when done, and before they are cold, with a sharp tin cutter stamp out the macaroons in the form of leaves, or crescents; bend these across a rolling-pin, and, when thoroughly cold and crisp, they may be removed, and kept in a box in a dry temperature.

STICKS OF VANILLA.

Ingredients: 4 oz. of sifted sugar, 4 oz. of flour, 4 yolks of eggs, 1½ oz. of butter dissolved, a tablespoonful of vanilla sugar.

First work the sugar, vanilla, and yolks of eggs, in a basin for ten minutes; then add the flour and the butter; work all together vigorously until well incorporated; fill a biscuit or macaroon forcer with some of the paste, using a tin piping-funnel, the point of which should be of the same width as a stick of vanilla; push out the paste on a table strewn with sifted sugar; cut the piping in four or five inch lengths, and lay these out straight, in rather close parallel rows upon a baking-sheet previously sparingly rubbed all over with white wax (the baking-sheet must be first warmed). When all the paste is laid out as directed, fill a paper *cornet* with royal icing strongly flavored with vanilla sugar, and push or pipe the icing upon these sticks of paste; when completed, push in the oven, moderate heat, and bake them of a light color.

STICKS OF CINNAMON.

Prepare the paste as in the preceding case, using cinnamon sugar instead of vanilla; and flavor the icing with cinnamon sugar also.

GENOESE PASTE.

The ingredients for making this paste are the same as for pound-cake; but, when intended to be converted into Genoese, the paste must be spread out on a baking-sheet lined with thin buttered paper. The thickness of the Genose depends entirely on the purpose for which it may be required: in any case, it must be baked of a light color.

Instructions will be hereafter given for a great variety of cakes, the foundation of which consists of this kind of paste.

CHAPTER III.

MASSEPAINS AND ALMOND-CAKES IN GENERAL.

MASSEPAINS, PLAIN.—MASSEPAINS SOUFFLÉS.—ORNAMENTAL ROUT-CAKES.—FILBERTS, FAGOTS, CARROTS, TURNIPS, WALNUTS, BALLS, HEARTS, RINGS, TREFOIL.—ALMOND CROCKETS, VARIOUS.—ALMOND CRACKLINGS, VARIOUS.—PISTACHIO MACAROONS.—FILBERT MACAROONS.—BRUSSELS MACAROONS.—MOIST MACAROONS.—DUTCH MACAROONS.—SPANISH MACAROONS.—VICTORIA MACAROONS.—CHOCOLATE MACAROONS.

MASSEPAINS, PLAIN.

INGREDIENTS: 12 oz. of sweet almonds, 1 oz. of bitter almonds, $1\frac{1}{2}$ lb. of sifted sugar, and 4 whites of eggs.

Scald, skin, wash, and dry the almonds, and pound them thoroughly in the mortar with the whites of eggs until thoroughly pulverized; then mix in the sugar by pounding, and take up the paste in a basin. Bear in mind that this must be kept *very firm;* and, in case it should be soft, add sugar enough to make it firmer.

Fill a macaroon-forcer with some of the paste, replace the wedge, and push out the *massepains* by directing the forcer along the table previously strewn with sifted sugar to prevent it from sticking; cut the forced ribs in lengths of two or three inches, twist them into shapes upon sheet wafer laid out upon baking-plates, and arrange the *massepains* in the form of rings, hearts, diamonds, spades, clubs, esses, triangles, and the figures 1, 2, 3, and 8; push them in the oven, and bake them of a *very* light color.

MASSEPAINS SOUFFLÉS.

Ingredients: 12 oz. of sweet almonds, 1 oz. of bitter almonds, 1½ lb. of sifted sugar, 1 oz. of vanilla sugar, 3 whites of eggs, and 1 white of egg of royal icing.

Prepare the paste as in the preceding case, and, when taken up in the basin, mix in the royal icing, remembering that this paste must be kept *quite firm*. Use a macaroon-forcer to push out the paste, and lay out the *massepains* upon sheet wafer in rings only; bake them in slack heat, of a very light color.

PASTE FOR ORNAMENTAL ROUT-CAKES.

Ingredients: 8 oz. of almonds cleaned, 8 oz. of sifted sugar, 1 oz. of flour, 4 yolks of eggs; flavor with any kind of essence.

Pound the almonds until thoroughly pulverized, adding occasionally a few drops of orange-flower, or plain water; then add the other ingredients; and when the whole has been well pounded into a very firm, smooth paste, take it up in a basin, and then proceed as indicated in the following articles.

FILBERT ROUT-CAKES.

Prepare the paste as in the preceding case; roll it out with sifted sugar upon the slab, to the thickness of the eighth of an inch, or rather thinner; use a tin-cutter to stamp out some leaves of the size, and as nearly as possible in the form, of the pointed or fringed hulls that surround a filbert; this is easily imitated by cutting or dividing one end of the leaves with the point of a knife: then take a large cleaned almond or filbert kernel, surround the bottom part of it with four of the prepared leaves, to be stuck and pinched together at the bottom in order to form the stem; stick or fasten two, three, or four of these filberts together so as to form a cluster; and, as you turn each cluster of filberts out of hand, set it firmly and uprightly upon a baking-sheet previously very thinly waxed over. When the whole or such part of the paste as may be intended for filberts is used up, set the cakes to dry in the screen until the next day, very moderate heat; the filberts are afterwards to be baked in slack heat until quite dry; *little* or *no* color. Next prepare one white of egg of royal icing; color two-thirds of this with spinach-green, and the remainder of a light nut-brown, with dissolved chocolate. Paint over the kernels with the brown color, and the leaves, but more especially their tips, with the green icing; remember that the green icing must be of a tender, delicate color: dry the filberts in the screen for a few minutes only, in order not to damage the color of the icing.

WALNUT ROUT-CAKES.

Prepare the paste as in preceding; leave one-third in its natural state, and color the remainder of a light brown with grated chocolate and ground cloves; use a cut board representing the model of half the shell of a walnut to push into the hollow form of the shell a small piece of the brown paste, and cut the surplus off level with the board: take out the model carefully, and place it with the flat part downwards upon a waxed baking-plate, to be dried, and afterwards baked. Use some of the uncolored paste to model the kernels in like manner; dry and bake these also; and, when both parts of the walnut are complete, stick them together so as to represent a walnut, the upper part of which has been shelled: they are then to be dried a little longer in the screen.

ALMOND FAGOT ROUT-CAKES.

Prepare the paste as in preceding, roll it out thin, cut it in bands measuring $1\frac{1}{4}$ inch in width, cut these in straw-like shreds, gather up a dozen of them in a straight bunch, tie them together with a shred of the same paste, and, as they are turned out of hand, place the fagots in rows upon a waxed baking-plate; dry them until the next day, and then bake them of a very light color.

ROUT-CAKES IN THE FORM OF CARROTS.

Prepare the paste as in previous cases, divide it into small pieces the size of a small walnut, fashion these with your hands by rolling them into the form of small spring carrots; insert a very small toothpick-like splinter of wood into the thick end of the carrot, tie a piece of thread in a loop to this, and, as they are turned out of hand, fasten them to a suspended piece of wire secured to two iron skewers stuck into a board, and place them in the screen to dry until the next day; afterwards to be placed upon a baking-plate and baked. The carrots are then to be dipped in red royal icing, and again suspended to the wire for the purpose of being dried; after which, take out the wooden skewers, and, in their stead, stick a piece of green angelica, using royal icing to fasten it in its place.

ROUT-CAKES IN THE FORM OF TURNIPS.

Use the paste indicated in the preceding article for the purpose of forming small spring turnips; dry these in the same manner as directed for spring carrots, ice them over with royal white icing, and, when dried, insert a few small shreds of green angelica at the thick end to represent the green tops of the turnips.

ROUT-CAKES IN THE FORM OF BALLS.

Stamp out two dozen or more small rounds of thin paste, and place them in rows on a waxed baking-plate; form some of the paste into small round balls the size of a nut, and place them, three and one, on the top of these, upon the centre of the rounds, with a twig of angelica stuck in between each ball; dry, and bake them of a light color, and paint them over with pink icing.

ROUT-CAKES IN THE FORM OF HEARTS, ETC.

Roll out some of the paste with the fingers upon the slab (using fine sugar to prevent it from sticking) into thin ropes; twist two of these together in the form of cords, and form with them hearts, rings, trefoils, diamonds, &c. Place them upon a waxed baking-plate; dry, and bake them of a light color, and use white and pink royal icing to pipe them over in ornamental designs.

ALMOND CROCKETS.

Ingredients: 8 oz. of flour, 8 oz. of almonds, 8 oz. of sugar, the zest of two oranges rasped on sugar, 2 whole eggs, and 1 yolk.

Do not scald the almonds, nor remove their hulls, but merely wipe off their dust, and pound them thoroughly in the mortar with a few drops of orange-flower water until reduced to a pulp; then mix in the remainder of the ingredients by pounding all together; take up the paste, knead it with a little flour upon the slab, roll it out in the shape of a rolling-pin; lay this on a greased baking-sheet, egg it over, and bake it in very moderate heat; when done, and while hot, cut it up in thin slices, and dry them on a baking-sheet in the oven; after they are dried, moisten their edges with royal icing, dip them in finely-chopped pistachio kernels, and dry them a few minutes.

ALMOND CROCKETS, ANOTHER WAY.

For this purpose, use the same ingredients as in the preceding case; mix all together, leaving the almonds whole; roll out the paste in the form of a rolling-pin, and, when baked in very moderate heat, cut it up in slices (while hot; for, if allowed to cool, it would be impossible to cut it at all), and color the edges with pink chopped almonds or pink granite sugar.

PISTACHIO CROCKETS.

Ingredients: 8 oz. of fresh bloomy pistachios, in their natural state, not scalded; 8 oz. of sugar, 8 oz. of flour, 2 whole eggs and 1 yolk, a teaspoonful of vanilla sugar.

Mix all the ingredients together (leaving the pistachios whole) into a firm paste, roll it out, bake it, and finish the crockets as in the preceding case.

FILBERT CROCKETS.

Proceed as directed for almond crockets, using filbert kernels instead of almonds for the purpose; flavor the paste with noyeau.

ALMOND CRACKLINGS.

Ingredients: 6 oz. of scalded almonds, cut in short shreds; 4 oz. of ground almonds, 10 oz. of sifted sugar, 2 whites of eggs, a few drops of essence of vanilla.

Mix these ingredients all together in a basin, and use a dessert-spoon to lay out the cracklings, of the size of a walnut, upon sheet-wafer spread on baking-plates. The cracklings should be placed one inch and a half apart from each other, slightly spread out with the tip of the finger dipped in water, and kept to a circular form, and a quarter of an inch in thickness: bake them in moderate heat, and of a light color.

PISTACHIO CRACKLINGS.

Ingredients: 6 oz. of shred pistachios, 4 oz. of pounded pistachios, 10 oz. of sifted sugar, 2 whites of eggs, a tablespoonful of vanilla sugar.

Thoroughly mix all the ingredients together in a basin, and afterwards lay out the cracklings as directed in the preceding case. These cracklings must be baked in slack or slow heat, on account of the color of the pistachios, which is apt to turn yellowish if exposed to great heat.

FILBERT CRACKLINGS.

The same proportions as for almond cracklings, using filbert-kernels instead of almonds for the purpose; flavor with noyeau.

PISTACHIO MACAROONS.

Ingredients: 4 oz. of bitter almonds, 12 oz. of sifted sugar, 6 oz. of shred pistachio kernels, a tablespoonful of vanilla sugar, and 2 whites of eggs.

Pound the bitter almonds with the whites of eggs until thoroughly pulverized; then mix the remainder of the ingredients with this in a basin; fill a biscuit-forcer with the preparation, and lay out the macaroons in round balls, the size of a walnut, upon sheet-wafer spread upon baking-sheets; push them in the oven at very moderate heat, and bake them without much color.

FILBERT MACAROONS.

Ingredients: 8 oz. of scalded filbert kernels, $1\frac{1}{4}$ lb. of sifted sugar, a few drops of essence of bitter almonds.

Pound the filberts with the essence and the whites of eggs, then mix in the sugar · the paste must be rather firm: roll the paste out in round balls the size of a small walnut; arrange them upon sheet-wafer laid on baking-sheets, and bake them of a light color.

BRUSSELS MACAROONS.

Ingredients: 3 oz. of sweet almonds, 3 oz. of bitter almonds, 8 oz. of sifted sugar, 2 whites of eggs of firm royal icing.

Pound the almonds thoroughly with a few drops of orange-flower water; take this up into a basin, and mix in with it the remainder of the ingredients; fill a biscuit-forcer with the composition, and lay out the macaroons upon sheet-wafer, about the size of a walnut, in an oval form; bake them in a slack oven, of a light color.

MOIST MACAROONS.

Ingredients: 8 oz. of sweet almonds, ¾ lb. of sugar, 1 oz. of chopped candied orange-peel, 1 oz. of chopped green angelica, 1 oz. of chopped candied orange-flowers, 2 whites of eggs, and 1 tablespoonful of double orange-flower water.

Pound the almonds with the orange-flower water; put this, with the sugar, into a sugar-boiler, and stir all together over the fire until the mixture begins to string as you hold up the spoon out of the pan; the paste must then be allowed to become partially cool, and then add the whites of eggs; mix thoroughly; push out the macaroons in an oval form, and bake them in very moderate heat.

DUTCH MACAROONS.

Ingredients: 6 oz. of ground almonds, 12 oz. of sifted sugar, 2 whites of eggs, a pinch of bruised coriander-seeds, ditto of ground cloves, some dried cherries, and angelica.

Pound the almonds with the whites of eggs; then add the sugar and the spice, and lay out the macaroons in the form of small fingers upon sheet-wafer, and place them in a warm temperature (not so hot as the screen) until the next day; you then press the back part of the blade of a knife straight down the centre, and on one-half of the macaroons (after they have been egged over) you insert a row of dried cherries, while down the centre of the remainder you insert a stripe of green angelica. Bake them in moderate heat.

SPANISH MACAROONS.

Ingredients: 8 oz. of sweet almonds, 1 lb. of sugar, 12 yolks of eggs, a teaspoonful of ground cinnamon, and the rasped rind of two oranges.

Boil the sugar to the blow degree; then add the pounded almonds and the flavoring, and allow them to simmer very gently together over a slow fire for ten minutes. By a slow fire, I mean a smothered charcoal fire, or some such kind of slow heat incapable of sufficient intensity to burn the composition. At the end of the ten minutes' gentle boiling (stirring occasionally), add the yolks of eggs, and stir the paste again over the fire (quicker heat) until it becomes both firm and compact: it must then be removed from the fire, and, when cooled, is to be rolled in the hands slightly greased with oil of sweet almonds, and laid out upon sheet-wafer spread on baking-sheets, and baked in rather sharp heat.

VICTORIA MACAROONS.

Ingredients: 8 oz. of burnt almonds, 10 oz. of sugar, 1 oz. candied orange-flowers, 2 whites of eggs.

Pound the almonds, the orange-flowers, and the whites of eggs, until nearly or coarsely pulverized; then mix in the sugar; keep the paste stiff, and lay out the macaroons in small ovals: bake them in moderate heat.

CHOCOLATE MACAROONS.

Ingredients: 12 oz. of ground almonds, 1½ lb. of sifted sugar, 4 oz. grated French chocolate, a tablespoonful of vanilla-sugar; 3 whites of eggs. Mix all the ingredients together, in a basin, into a stiff paste, and lay out the macaroons upon sheet-wafer in the form of short fingers: bake them in very moderate heat.

CHAPTER IV

ALMOND SOUFFLÉ ROUT-CAKES.

Frascati Croquantes. — Small Soufflés in Cases. — Small Soufflés of Pistachios. — Small Soufflés with Chocolate. — Diavolini. — Small Soufflés with Candied Peels. — Zephyr Soufflés. — Zephyr Soufflés with Pistachios. — Zephyr Soufflés, Rose-Pink. — Almond Soufflés. — Pistachio Soufflés.

FRASCATI CROQUANTES.

Ingredients : 8 oz. of flour, 6 oz. of sugar, 2 oz. of ground almonds, 2 whole eggs and 3 yolks, $\frac{1}{2}$ oz. of anise-seed.

Whisk the eggs, almonds, and the sugar in a basin for ten minutes; then add the flour and the anise-seed, and work all together until thoroughly incorporated. Next roll out the paste, with flour on the slab, in the form of a long, thick rope, and use a knife to divide it in pieces the size of a walnut; roll each in the palm of your hand with the fingers into ovals, or round balls; place these in rows upon a buttered baking-sheet; press the back of a knife across their surfaces, so as to effect a slight incision; egg them over, sprinkle rough-grained or granite sugar upon them, and bake them in moderate heat.

SMALL SOUFFLÉS IN CASES.

Ingredients: 4 whites of eggs, 12 oz. of sifted sugar, 2 oz. of candied orange-flowers.

Whisk the whites of eggs perfectly stiff, and then use a tablespoon to incorporate the sugar and slightly bruised orange-flowers; use a teaspoon to fill small paper cases with this paste, bearing in mind that the cases must not be more than three parts filled, as, from its extreme lightness, the paste is very liable to run over the sides. Bake in slow heat.

SMALL SOUFFLÉS OF PISTACHIOS.

Ingredients : 4 whites of eggs, 12 oz. of sifted sugar, 2 oz. of shred pistachios, a tablespoonful of vanilla-sugar.

Proceed as indicated in the foregoing.

SMALL SOUFFLÉS WITH CHOCOLATE.

Ingredients : 4 whites of eggs, 12 oz. of sifted sugar, 2 oz. of grated chocolate, a tablespoonful of vanilla-sugar.

Proceed as directed in preceding.

DIAVOLINI.

Ingredients : 1 oz. of gum-dragon, about $1\frac{1}{2}$ lb. of fine sifted icing-sugar, a dessert-spoonful of essence of cinnamon, and a dessert-spoonful of essence of Jamaica ginger.

First wash the gum, and then put it to soak, with a gill of tepid water, in a covered gallipot; when the gum has absorbed all the water, it will have become sufficiently soft to admit of its being easily squeezed, or rather wrung through a strong clean cloth upon a plate : work this gum with your flattened fist on a slab, adding the sugar gradually until the paste becomes stiff enough to enable you to handle it : you now add the two essences, and work in the remainder of the sugar; and, if the quantity named should prove insufficient to produce a very stiff paste, add more sugar, as possibly the gum may have been too much diluted. Keep the Diavolini paste in a covered pot while you are using it. The Diavolini are shaped in the following manner :—

Take a piece of the paste the size of a walnut, roll it out with your hands, with fine sugar strewn on the slab, so as to form it into a rope about the eighth of an inch thick; divide this with a knife into very small dots, and use fine sugar to aid in rolling them with your finger against the palm of your hand, so as to shape each in the form of a grain of rye or barley. As the Diavolini are turned out of hand, they should be dropped into a clean dry sieve containing half an inch deep of fine dry icing-sugar, and, when a certain number of Diavolini is completed, move the sieve to and fro to riddle off the sugar; strew them apart from each other over a sheet of paper on a baking-plate, and dry them in the screen; moderate heat.

Use up the whole of the paste in this manner, and, when the Diavolini are thoroughly dry and cold, keep them in airtight stoppered bottles.

NOTE. — These comfits are very expensive to buy, and are, moreover, very seldom to be met with in any of the confectioners' shops. I have placed them here on account of their being required to complete the following recipe.

SMALL SOUFFLÉS WITH CANDIED PEELS:

Ingredients: 4 whites of eggs, 12 oz. of sifted sugar, 1 oz. of Diavolini, and 2 oz. of finely shred candied peels.

Whisk the whites stiff, then incorporate the sugar, Diavolini, and peels; nearly fill the small paper cases, and bake the soufflés, in slow heat, of a very light color.

ZEPHYR SOUFFLÉS.

Ingredients: 8 oz. of fine sifted sugar, 8 oz. of finely shred almonds, 2 whites of eggs, and a few drops of essence of peppermint.

Put the whites of eggs and the sugar in an untinned copper sugar-boiler, and whisk them over a very slow smothered charcoal stove fire into a substantial white frothy icing; you then add the almonds, and about three drops of the essence, and gently mix the whole with a dessert-spoon; then lay out the zephyrs in the manner following:—

Spread some sheets of white wafer upon baking-plates, and use a dessert-spoon to lay out the zephyrs in lumps the size of a rather large walnut, one nch and a half apart from each other; bake them, in slow heat, of a very light color.

ZEPHYRS WITH PISTACHIOS.

Ingredients: 4 whites of eggs, 8 oz. of sifted sugar, 8 oz. of finely shred pistachios, and a few drops of essence of vanilla or orange-flower water.

Whisk the whites of eggs stiff, incorporate the sugar, pistachios, and essence lightly, and lay out, and bake the zephyrs as directed in the preceding case.

These zephyrs must be dredged over with sugar previously to their being put into the oven.

ZEPHYRS, ROSE-PINK.

Ingredients: 4 whites of eggs, 8 oz. of sifted sugar, 8 oz. of shred filberts or cleansed walnut-kernels, a few drops of essence of roses, and a few drops of prepared cochineal.

Proceed in all particulars as indicated in the foregoing.

ALMOND SOUFFLÉS.

Ingredients: 8 oz. of sweet almonds, 1 oz. of bitter almonds, 1½ lb. of very fine sifted icing-sugar, about 3 whites of eggs, any kind of flavoring, such as orange, lemon, vanilla, or essence of cinnamon; the flavoring must be added to 2 whites of eggs of royal icing, required to finish the soufflés.

Scald, skin, wash, wipe, and dry the almonds in the screen; next pound them with about two ounces of the sugar, adding occasionally some of the white of eggs until reduced to a smooth pulp; then incorporate the remainder of the sugar by working it into the paste on the slab with clean hands. Bear in mind that this paste is to be kept rather stiff.

Roll out the paste with sugar on the slab to the thickness of a quarter of an inch; spread the icing evenly upon this, and use either tin cutters or a knife to stamp or cut out rings, esses, crescents, trefoil, diamonds, hearts, spades, &c.;

or else, in order to occasion no waste, merely cut out small squares, oblongs, lozenges, and triangles. Place the cakes, as they are stamped or cut out, upon sheet-wafer laid on baking-plates, and bake them in slow heat, *very* light color.

PISTACHIO SOUFFLÉS.

Ingredients: 10 oz. of pistachios, 1½ lb. of fine sugar, 3 whites of eggs, a few drops of essence of roses, 2 whites of eggs of royal rose-pink icing.

Proceed as in the foregoing case.

CHAPTER V

CAKES, JUMBLES, &c.

SPONGE-CAKE. — CUP-CAKE. — QUEEN-CAKE. — JUMBLES. — JELLY-CAKE. — KISSES. — COCOANUT-CAKE.   LADY-CAKE. — CHARLOTTE RUSSE.

SPONGE-CAKE.

Take 1 lb. of eggs, and an extra one to allow for the egg shells, 1 lb. sifted powdered sugar, $\frac{1}{2}$ lb. of flour, the juice and rind of 1 lemon. Separate the yolks of the eggs from the whites. Beat the sugar into the yolks till it is as light as possible, then beat the whites and add them; stir the flour in gently, only enough to mix thoroughly, and bake in a quick oven.

CUP-CAKE.

Take 1 cup of butter, 2 of sugar, 4 of flour, 1 of sour cream, and 3 eggs, with a little brandy and rose-water. Beat the eggs well, then add the other things as in poundcake. Have ready dissolved in a little sweet milk a half teaspoonful of cake soda, and pour in at the last; being careful that no lumps of the soda shall go in: then beat well for a few minutes, and bake at once in little tins or cups, well buttered, only half filled.

QUEEN-CAKE.

1 lb. of flour, 1 lb. sifted sugar, 1 lb. currants, 1 lb. butter, 1 tea-cup of cream, 8 eggs, yolks and whites beaten separately; add rose-water to flavor, and beat well as for pound-cake. Bake them in little tins, as for cup-cake.

JUMBLES.

Rub 1 lb. of butter into 1¼ lb. of flour; beat 4 eggs with 1¼ lb. of sugar; when very light, mix with the butter and flour. Stir in a wine-glass of rose-water; roll them out on a pie-board, and cut them into rings. Bake slowly, and, when brown, take them out, and sift powdered sugar over them.

JELLY-CAKE.

This cake may be made by the receipts for sponge or cup cake. Have shallow tin pans or plates of the same size, butter them, and pour in the batter so as to be about half an inch thick when baked; they bake in a few minutes of a light-brown, and, as you take them from the oven, lay them on a flat surface, spreading a layer of jelly on the top; then pile them until you have it thick enough, so that the jelly is between each two cakes; reserve the nicest-looking cake for the top, which must be left without jelly. It may be sugared with sifted sugar: cut in slices before serving. Grape or currant jelly is best for the purpose.

KISSES.

Beat the whites of eight eggs until very light, then sift in gradually one pound of powdered sugar; add a little lemon-juice and essence, or rose-brandy, to flavor: when it is well beaten, drop it by the spoonful on sheets of white paper, not near enough to touch, and bake in a moderate oven until a light-brown.

COCOANUT-CAKE.

Pare off the brown skin from the white cocoanut, and then grate into a plate. Beat together the whites of four eggs and half a pound of sifted sugar with a little rose-water. Stir into this the grated cocoanut until it becomes very stiff; then take up a pinch with the thumb and finger, and form it into a little cone; place these on a sheet of white paper, and bake in a moderate oven until brown.

LADY-CAKE.

Made like pound-cake, only using the whites of eggs alone.

CHARLOTTE RUSSE.

To half a pint of milk put one ounce of isinglass, or Cox's gelatine; to this add a vanilla-bean; let it simmer over the fire. Beat the whites of four eggs to a stiff froth, stir the yolks thoroughly with three ounces of pulverized sugar and one pint of thick cream, with one wine-glass full of white wine, to a complete froth. When the isinglass is dissolved, strain the milk, while lukewarm, into the yolks and sugar, add the whites immediately, next the cream; beat all together. Then line the mould with strips of sponge-cake, or lady-fingers, pour over the mixture, and let it stand in a cold place until perfectly firm, when it may be turned out into a glass dish.

ANOTHER RECEIPT FOR CHARLOTTE RUSSE.

Take 1 quart of cream, 1 tea-cup of sifted powdered sugar, 3 tablespoonfuls of brandy, 1 tablespoonful of vanilla. Put all in a three-quart tin pail with *ice* or *snow* packed around it. Beat to a stiff froth, which will take from *twenty to thirty minutes*. Put four sheets of isinglass in a gill of water; let it simmer over the fire until all is dissolved, then strain and let it get quite cool, pour slowly into the beaten cream, beating gently all the time, that it may be thoroughly mixed. Pour in a mould (or common deep cake pan), lined with sponge-cake, and put on the ice.

Try it. The cream pie sponge cake is very nice for it.

CHAPTER VI.

DESSERT WAFERS IN GENERAL.

Italian Wafers. — French Wafers. — Flemish Gauffres. — French Gauffres. — Spanish Wafers. — Ginger Wafers.

ITALIAN WAFERS.

Ingredients: 8 oz. of sifted sugar, 8 oz. of flour, 2 eggs, ½ a gill of orange-flower water, ½ pint of milk, 2 oz. butter, a pinch of salt.

Place the flour, sugar, salt, orange-flower water, eggs, and the milk in a pan, and vigorously work all together with a wooden spoon; then add the dissolved butter, and work the batter for ten minutes longer. While you are preparing the batter, you will have heated the wafer-irons over a clear charcoal stove-fire, bearing in mind that they must be frequently turned over in order that they may be equally heated in every part: when sufficiently hot, rub them inside with a paste-brush dipped in clarified butter, pour a good tablespoonful of the butter on the bottom or under sheet of the wafer-irons; close the top part upon this, and bake the wafers on both sides. They must be of a very light-fawn color, and, when done, are to be immediately rolled into shape upon a stick made for the purpose, measuring about five inches long by one inch in the thickness or diameter. The first wafer baked serves only thoroughly to cleanse the irons, and to ascertain their degree of heat. If the wafer turns out pale and soft, the irons are not hot; if, on the contrary, the wafer has too much color, allow the irons to cool for a minute or two before you attempt to bake any more. Keep these wafers in a closed tin box, in a warm temperature, for use as occasion requires.

FRENCH WAFERS.

Ingredients : 8 oz. of flour, 8 oz. of sifted sugar, a tablespoonful of vanilla-sugar, a pinch of salt, a wineglassful of brandy, 4 whites of eggs, ½ pint of single cream.

Work the flour, sugar, flavoring, salt, whites of eggs, and cream in a basin, with a whisk, into a smooth batter; then add the brandy, and again work all vigorously together for ten minutes. These wafers are to be baked and curled on wooden pillars or rollers, in the manner described in the preceding.

FLEMISH GAUFFRÈS.

Ingredients : 12 oz. of flour, 6 oz. of butter, 6 eggs, 1 pint of milk, 1 oz. of good yeast, a glass of kirschenwasser, the rind of 2 oranges rubbed on sugar and scraped off, ¼ oz. of salt.

Place the flour in a large pan, add the yeast dissolved with a spoonful of hot water, then the salt and the eggs, and work all together; next add the milk made lukewarm, and, as soon as this is incorporated, add the dissolved butter, and work the batter vigorously for ten minutes; pass a knife round the sides of the pan; throw a cloth over it, and set it in the screen (if not too hot), that the batter may rise: this will be effected in about three-quarters of an hour. The gauffres are then to be baked in gauffre-irons, which said gauffre-irons are to be heated over a clear charcoal stove-fire, and, when hot, to be brushed inside with a little clarified butter, a large spoonful of the batter poured into the under sheet of the gauffre-irons, then closed in and baked on both sides. These gauffres should be of a golden-brown color, and when finished and cut in squares, according to their apparent divisions, should be sprinkled over with sugar, to be served either for luncheon, tea, or coffee.

FRENCH GAUFFRES.

Ingredients: 9 oz. of flour, 4 oz. of sifted sugar, 8 eggs, a spoonful of vanilla-sugar, a pinch of salt, a wineglassful of noyeau, and a pint of whipped cream.

Place the flour, sugar, salt, vanilla, noyeau, and yolks of eggs, in a pan, and thoroughly work all together until well mixed; then add the whites of eggs and the whipped cream: mix all lightly together, taking care that the whole of the ingredients are thoroughly incorporated. Bake the gauffres as directed in the preceding, but with less color: they are well adapted, from their lightness and crispness, to be handed round with ices, if only for a change, instead of the old-fashioned wafers.

SPANISH WAFERS.

Ingredients: 9 oz. of flour, 2 oz. of sifted sugar, half a pint of water chocolate (consisting of 2 oz. of French or Spanish chocolate dissolved in ½ pint of boiling water, and milled), a few drops of essence of vanilla, 2 eggs, and a gill of cream.

Place the flour, sugar, vanilla, eggs, and the cream in a pan, and vigorously work all together into a smooth elastic batter; then add the chocolate cold, whisk all together for ten minutes, and bake the wafers as directed; when done, curl them in the form of cornucopiæ, using a wooden form or mandrin upon which to shape the wafers. Such tools are obtainable at all turners.

GINGER WAFERS.

Ingredients: 8 oz. of flour, 1 pint of single cream, 4 oz. of treacle, a teaspoonful of essence of ginger, 2 oz. of butter, a pinch of salt.

Mix thoroughly the above ingredients in a stewpan, and stir them, while boiling, quickly on the fire for three minutes, and then bake the wafers in manner following:—

Take a copper baking-sheet scoured bright on the untinned side, or under part, and place this side uppermost over a clear charcoal stove-fire, that it may become sufficiently heated for your purpose; that is, moderately heated.

You now drop a tablespoonful of the batter in two or three places on the heated baking-sheet, and spread it out, with the back part of the bowl of the spoon, to the size of a small saucer, and, as bubbles rise on the surface, flatten them with the tip of the spoon. As soon as the wafers become a little dry and crisp, slip a long-bladed sharp knife carefully under, to detach them; and, as you do so, hand them to another person, that they may be instantly curled on the several pointed wooden mandrins used to give the shape of a cornucopia, or pointed sugar-bag, such as grocers use to wrap up some of their goods in small quantities.

These wafers must be kept in a dry place, yet not too hot: when made small, they may be filled with whipped cream, with a strawberry placed on the top.

CHAPTER VII.

LONG BISCUITS ICED, AND DIFFERENT SORTS OF MERINGUES.

GENERAL REMARKS ON MERINGUES.—ORDINARY MERINGUES.—CREAM-ICED MERINGUES.—MERINGUES WITH PRESERVE.—ITALIAN MERINGUES.—ITALIAN MERINGUES GARNISHED.—ICED ITALIAN MERINGUES.—MERINGUES IN THE FORM OF CAULIFLOWERS.—MERINGUES IN THE FORM OF MUSHROOMS.—MERINGUES IN THE FORM OF STRAWBERRIES.—MERINGUES IN THE FORM OF GRAPES.—LONG OBTUSE-POINTED BISCUITS ICED WITH CHOCOLATE.—LONG OBTUSE-POINTED BISCUITS WITH ROSE-PINK ICING.—LONG OBTUSE-POINTED BISCUITS WITH WHITE ICING.—LONG OBTUSE-POINTED BISCUITS WITH SPINACH-GREEN ICING.—LONG OBTUSE-POINTED BISCUITS WITH COFFEE ICING.

GENERAL REMARKS ON MERINGUES.

IT is impossible to bake meringues properly without using for the purpose what are called meringue-boards. These should be made of well-seasoned hard-wood, with rounded corners, and of convenient size for your oven: they must be about one and a half inches thick.

As meringues, while being baked, must remain soft underneath, the boards must be thoroughly damped with water previously to placing the bands of paper containing the meringues upon them. By this precaution, the meringues are effectually prevented from receiving any considerable amount of heat capable of rendering them at all hard underneath.

ORDINARY MERINGUES.

Ingredients: 1 lb. of sifted sugar, and 12 whites of eggs perfectly free from any the least particle of the yolks.

Whisk the whites, in a copper egg-bowl, into a very stiff snowy froth, and then mix in the sugar gradually, lightly, yet thoroughly incorporated, using a spoon for this purpose; and proceed to lay out the meringues according to the following directions :—

Cut some sheets of stout foolscap paper into bands measuring two inches in width; then take a tablespoon and gather it nearly full of the composition by working it up at the side of the bowl in the form of an egg, and drop this slopingly upon the end of one of the bands of paper, at the same time drawing the edge of the spoon sharply round the base of the meringue, so as to give it a smooth and rounded appearance resembling an egg; fill the band of paper with a row of meringues, kept at an inch distance from each other. As each band is so filled, place them close beside each other upon the table; and, when all are completed, dredge sifted sugar all over them. After allowing them to remain in this state for three minutes, take hold of the bands at each end, shake off the excess of loose sugar, and place the bands in close rows upon the wetted boards : as soon as the sugar begins to dissolve on their surface, push them in the oven (very moderate heat), and bake them of a very light fawn color.

When the meringues are done, remove each piece separately and carefully off the paper : use a dessert-spoon to scoop out the white soft part, and with the point of the bowl of the spoon smooth the inside of the meringues; after this they are to be placed with the rounded side downwards upon baking-sheets to dry the insides in the oven, and, when thoroughly crisp, are to be kept between sheets of paper in a tin box in a very dry place. When using the meringues for dessert or otherwise, garnish them with whipped cream flavored with vanilla, orange, lemon, or any other flavored sugar, with orange-flower water, or any kind of liqueur, sticking two halves together after they are so garnished. These *meringues* may also be slightly garnished with any kind of preserve previously to adding the whipped cream.

CREAM-ICED MERINGUES.

For this purpose the *meringues* should be made smaller, about the size of a pigeon's egg: they are to be filled very neatly with stiff whipped cream, taking care that when the two halves are closed together none of the cream is allowed to ooze over the edges; or, if it should do so, wipe it off. When the meringues are ready crammed, hold each separately on a silver fork to dip them all over in transparent icing, using for the purpose any of those before described.

CREAM-ICED MERINGUES WITH PRESERVES

Are to be prepared as indicated in the preceding case, with some kind of preserve added, which is to be thinly spread inside the meringues before garnishing them with the cream.

ITALIAN MERINGUES.

Ingredients: $1\frac{1}{4}$ lb. of sugar, 4 whites of eggs, and any kind of flavoring.

Boil the sugar to the blow degree, and then set the sugar-boiler standing in a soup-plate containing cold water. Whip the whites of eggs into a stiff snowy froth; and having worked the sugar with the back part of the bowl of a table-spoon continuously up against the sides of the pan, fetching it up from the bottom at the same time, in order that the whole of the sugar may be equally worked so as to become semi-opalized, add the whipped whites, and afterwards the juice of a lemon, and a liqueur-glass of any kind of liqueur, and thoroughly, though lightly, mix all together. You will find, that, as the paste cools, it will become sufficiently firm to enable you to lay it out in a similar manner to that described for the moulding of ordinary meringues, excepting that, as a general rule, Italian *meringues* should be small. They are susceptible of being made in almost an infinite variety of forms; using, in that case, a biscuit-forcer for the purpose of shaping the meringues to represent hearts, rings, crescents, diamonds, trefoil, grapes, and other fruits, &c. This meringue-paste may be colored rose-pink by adding a few drops of cochineal, yellow with saffron, brown with chocolate. Italian meringues require to be dried only, rather than baked: due care must therefore be taken, previously to using the oven for this purpose, to ascertain that the heat is not sufficient to color a piece of white paper.

As the proportion of sugar contained in the Italian meringue is greater than in the ordinary meringue, it does not require dredging after being shaped, possessing already sufficient consistency; yet, when fruits or vegetables are intended to be imitated, different colored granite sugars are sprinkled on their surface to effect such resemblance. In all ordinary cases, when not desirable to ornament, or in any way vary the original color of the Italian meringues, as soon as their surfaces have become sufficiently dry to admit of a slight pressure of the finger without giving way, remove them from the oven, and use a broad-bladed knife having a rounded tip, with which to lift the meringues off their paper; the first half so lifted to be laid upon its back in the palm of your left hand, gently withdrawing the knife without damaging its form; and then, as you remove the fellow-half from the paper, and place it upon that already in your left hand, gently press both together, and set the perfect ring, heart, &c., out of hand upon a wire tray, to be further dried for a few minutes.

ITALIAN MERINGUES GARNISHED.

For this purpose, the paste, prepared as in the preceding, should be laid out in the form and of the size of a pigeon's egg. When the meringues are dry, and previously to sticking the two halves together, use a teaspoon to scoop out a portion of their interiors, thus leaving a hollow to be filled up with whipped cream and any kind of small fresh fruit or preserve, and then to be closed, and allowed to become hardened or dried, without any further exposure to heat of any kind, as this would necessarily melt the cream, and consequently defeat the desired purpose.

ITALIAN MERINGUES COVERED WITH TRANSPARENT ICING.

Prepare the meringues as directed in the preceding case, and afterwards use a fork, upon which they are to be placed for the purpose of dipping them in any of the transparent icings described in this work.

The advantage of Italian meringues, when these are intended to be covered with icing, consists in their possessing greater substance than ordinary meringues; although it must be admitted that the latter, in one sense at least, are better adapted for the purpose, from their superior delicacy.

MERINGUES IN THE FORM OF CAULIFLOWERS.

Fill a biscuit-forcer with Italian meringue-paste, and push this out upon bands of paper, in knobs, or large dots, superposed or mounted one upon the other in such form or fashion, that, when complete, it shall represent, as nearly as possible, the head, or white part, of a cauliflower (of course, on a very diminished scale, of the size of a pigeon's egg, for instance): this part of the cauliflower, when fashioned, is to be sprinkled over with rather coarse granite sugar. The under part, or green leaves, which envelop a cauliflower, are imitated in a somewhat similar manner to the above by pushing out the paste in pointed dots upon bands of paper, in the manner and form as directed for the imitation of the heads, only somewhat flatter: these, in order the better to represent green leaves, are to be sprinkled over with green granite sugar; and when both parts have been dried in the closet, or screen, stick the head, or white part, upon the leafy or green part; thus you will form more or less truthful imitation of a cauliflower, according as in a greater or lesser degree you may have displayed your taste.

Patience, industry, and perseverance overcome all difficulties.

IMITATION MUSHROOMS.

Use a biscuit-forcer to push out the Italian meringue paste in the forms of small, long corks and round drops on stiff paper; slightly sprinkle these over with grated chocolate, and dry them in the closet, or screen; afterwards stick two of the elongated pieces resembling corks together, thus representing the stalks; run the narrowest end of these into the underpart of the drops; and by this means the mushroom will be imitated. The broad end, or base, of the stalk of the mushrooms, should be first dipped in white of egg, and then in grated chocolate, in order the more perfectly to imitate Nature by adding, as a last touch, the imitation of the dark mould which adheres to the stalks.

IMITATION STRAWBERRIES.

First push out any given number of large pointed dots, resembling as nearly as possible strawberries; sprinkle these over with rather coarse granite sugar composed of five parts of deep-pink color and one-sixth part yellow, well mixed. The leafy stalks of the fruit are to be imitated by using a small *cornet*, or paper biscuit-forcer, to pipe or push out small circular rows of pointed dots upon paper, which are to be sprinkled over with green granite sugar. When both strawberry and leaves are sufficiently dried, let the strawberries be stuck in the centre of the imitation of their leafy stalks.

IMITATION OF GRAPES.

As you prepare the Italian meringue, give it a rose-pink blush tint of color by adding a few drops of prepared cochineal, and use this paste to fill a biscuit-forcer with which to form the bunches of grapes by pushing out the meringue-paste in drops or pearls of different sizes, so grouped and arranged on the bands of paper as to represent small bunches of grapes. Intelligence and practice are, of course, needed to arrive at any degree of perfection in this as in every thing else. Try, and persevere. The leaves and stalks are easily imitated by cutting thin lozenges, or, as they are commonly called, diamonds, of green angelica; and, by placing five of these with the points of one end converging towards the stalk of the bunch of grapes, you will, to a certain extent, imitate the leaf. Stick a thin shred of angelica in at the base of this for the stalk.

LONG OBTUSE-POINTED BISCUITS WITH TRANSPARENT ICING.

This kind of dessert-cakes is very advantageous for dressing up those dessert side-dishes known to professional confectioners under the name of *drums*. They must be so placed as to present and show off the beautiful transparent *glacé* of their whole surface. Their very shape, resembling exactly the champagne biscuit-moulds, will at once show how easily they may be dished up according to the foregoing instructions.

Prepare and bake some sponge or other cake in a deep baking-sheet, about three-quarters of an inch in thickness, and, when cold, cut it up as directed above; trim neatly with a very sharp knife, and brush off every the least particle of crumbs, in order that the icing may not be prevented from adhering to the cake, and otherwise gain a rough or uneven surface. Carefully spread the upper part and sides of the biscuits with apricot jam; hold one at a time safely on a silver fork in the left hand, while, with a spoon in the right hand, you pour some transparent chocolate-icing all over the surface of the biscuit: when complete, place it carefully out of hand upon a wire tray resting on a baking-plate. As soon as the operation is terminated, dry the biscuits in the screen for five minutes.

MARBLED GLACÉS.

Place the sheet of biscuit on a baking-plate; drop different sized lumps of fine preserves, consisting of bright apricot jam, greengage jam, damson jam, white-apple jelly, and red-currant jelly; spread these smoothly so as to form a marbled pattern, and then cut out the cakes in any fancy shape; mask these over with colorless transparent icing, and dry them in the screen for five minutes. These very beautiful cakes tend considerably to enhance the elegance of a fashionable dessert.

GLACÉS WITH ROSE-PINK ICING.

Cut up the sponge or other cake in any fancy shapes of equal size; spread their surface with bright jelly, and mask them over with rose-pink transparent icing.

GLACÉS WITH WHITE TRANSPARENT ICING.

Proceed as indicated in the preceding, using white icing instead of pink.

GLACÉS WITH GREEN TRANSPARENT ICING.

Spread the drops or cakes with greengage jam, and mask them over with transparent icing colored with extract of spinach.

GLACÉS WITH TRANSPARENT COFFEE ICING.

Spread the sponge or other cake with a thin coating of apple jelly, and mask them with transparent icing flavored with coffee.

CHAPTER VIII.

DIFFERENT KINDS OF NOUGAT, PASTAFROLLE, AND CHESTNUT BISCUITS.

ORDINARY NOUGAT. — PARISIAN NOUGATS. — NOUGAT DE MARSEILLES. — TORONI BIANCA. — TORONI ROSSA. — TORONI WITH PISTACHIOS. — PASTAFROLLE. — NEAPOLITAN GLACÉS, WHITE. — NEAPOLITAN CAKE. — NEAPOLITAN GLACÉS WITH CHOCOLATE. — BONBON TARTLETS, ROSE-PINK. — BONBON TARTLETS, WHITE. — BONBON TARTLETS WITH CHOCOLATE. — BONBON TARTLETS OF GREENGAGE. — BONBON TARTLETS OF APRICOT. — BONBON ALMOND-PASTE ROUT-CAKES.

ORDINARY NOUGAT.

INGREDIENTS : 1 lb. of shred almonds dried, and 10 oz. of sifted sugar.

First put the almonds on a baking-plate just at the entrance of the open oven to make them hot through; and, while the almonds are being heated, place the sugar in a copper egg-bowl, and keep moving it about with a clean wooden spoon over a moderate stove-fire until it begins to melt; you then quicken the motion of the hand, and, as soon as you perceive that the sugar begins to pearl up on the surface in the form of small white bubbles, immediately throw in the almonds; stir all together gently until well mixed, and then proceed to use the *nougat* to line thinly small, deep, fancy-shaped moulds previously very slightly oiled inside. As each mould is so lined, cut the edges level before the nougat becomes quite cold; for it is then brittle, and breaks. A dozen or more of these small nougats, with an ornamental caramel sugar handle adapted to it, and afterwards filled with whipped cream and a strawberry at the top of each basket, form a very charming garnish for a dessert *drum* or side-dish.

PARISIAN NOUGATS.

Ingredients: 8 oz. of scalded and split pistachio-kernels, 6 oz. of sugar, and a few drops of essence of vanilla or a teaspoonful of vanilla-sugar, and a few drops of prepared cochineal.

Boil the sugar to the crack, then add the pistachios, the cochineal, and the flavoring; mix gently, and spread the nougat out flat upon a baking-sheet very slightly oiled to prevent it from sticking. A hard lemon slightly oiled should be used to flatten out the nougat to about the sixth of an inch in thickness; and, before it cools, let it be sprinkled over with small nibs of rough broken sugar free from its dust, and cleaned grocer's currants: press these on with the fingers, and divide the sheet of nougat, while hot, in small oblongs or diamonds, measuring about two and a half inches long by one inch in width. These nougats form a pretty variety for dessert.

NOUGAT DE MARSEILLES.

Ingredients: 8 oz. of honey, 8 oz. of sugar, 1¼ lb. of scalded and skinned almonds, ½ a gill of orange-flower water, 6 sheets of white wafer, and 3 whites of eggs whipped to a stiff snowy froth.

Melt and skim the honey, boil the sugar to the crack, add the honey and the orange-flower water, stir all together, and then add this by degrees to the whipped whites of eggs in the egg-bowl, stirring quickly as the sugar, &c., are poured into the whites: continue stirring this paste over a slow charcoal stove-fire, kept up at an equal degree of very moderate heat, until the paste attains to a sufficient consistency to arrive at that point, when, by dropping the value of a nut-size portion into cold water, it may, as it cools, be easily snapped or broken in two: this baking of the paste requires some three hours' strict attention. The almonds must now be added; and as soon as all is mixed, spread out the paste, about an inch thick and perfectly smooth, upon three of the sheets of wafer previously placed upon a sheet of paper laid on a baking-plate; cover this with the remaining three sheets of wafer; lay white paper on the top, and over all place a baking-plate with which to press the nougat level, and allow it to become cold. When required for use, this kind of nougat should be cut in oblong squares measuring one and a half inches long by one inch wide, and one-quarter of an inch in thickness. The color is of a light-brown.

TORONI BIANCA.

Ingredients: 8 oz. of sifted sugar, 8 oz. of thinly sliced filberts, 2 whites of eggs, and a spoonful of orange-flower water.

Place the sugar, whites of eggs, and the orange-flower water in a copper egg-bowl, and whisk the whole over a very slow fire until it attains to the consistency of ordinary meringue paste; you then add the shred filberts; stir all together, and lay out the nougat paste in the form of small ovals upon sheets of wafer on a baking-plate; bake, or rather dry, these in the oven, very moderate heat. These nougats must remain as white as possible.

TORONI ROSSA.

Ingredients: 8 oz. of almonds shred short, 8 oz. of sugar sifted, 3 whites of eggs, a tablespoonful of vanilla-sugar, a few drops of prepared cochineal, and 2 oz. of shred candied orange-peel.

Proceed as in the foregoing case, adding the almonds, orange-peel, vanilla, and cochineal last; spread out the nougat paste an inch thick upon two sheets of wafer; cover these with another two sheets of wafer; use a plate to press them level, and bake them in moderate heat, and, when nearly cold, cut them up in small thin oblong squares.

PISTACHIO TORONI.

Ingredients: 8 oz. of fresh purple skinned pistachios, 8 oz. of sifted sugar, 3 whites of eggs, and 1 oz. of candied orange-flowers.

Proceed in all respects as indicated for the preparation of toroni bianca.

PASTAFROLLE.

Ingredients: 9 oz. of flour, 6 oz. of sugar, 3 oz. of butter, 5 yolks of eggs, 4 oz. of sweet almonds, and 10 bitter almonds pounded smooth, with the white of an egg.

First work the butter with a spoon in a basin into a creamy substance, then work in the sugar and the yolks of eggs, afterwards the pounded almonds, and lastly the flour; knead the paste well together with a little flour on the slab.

NEAPOLITAN GLACÉS, WHITE.

Prepare the paste as in the foregoing; roll it out thin; stamp out any given number of small, round, oval, square, oblong, or any other fancy-shaped flats; place these in rows on thinly buttered baking-plates, and bake them in moderate heat: when done, stick two together with any kind of preserve, and *glacez* them over with any kind of transparent icing. These cakes may be decorated with ornamental piping.

A NEAPOLITAN CAKE.

Prepare the pastafrolle as directed; roll it out thin, stamp out twenty-four circular flats, measuring about five inches in diameter, — that is, five inches across, — bake these upon buttered baking-sheets in moderate heat, and, when done, press them flat on the slab with a dish containing a fourteen-pound weight upon it. The whole of the twenty-four flats are to be laid upon each other, stuck together with jam between each, so as to form a firm pile, representing one cake; trim the sides level and smooth, mask the whole surface with apricot jam, and decorate the cake with some elegant design formed with royal icing diped over it. This kind of cake is well adapted for a dessert dish.

NEAPOLITAN PASTAFROLLE ICED WITH CHOCOLATE.

Prepare the small flats as shown in the preceding, stick them together in the same manner, and *glacez* them over with transparent chocolate icing. These cakes may also be *glacés* with every variety of icing described in this book.

BONBON TARTLETS, ROSE-PINK.

Prepare some almond-paste, roll this out very thin with sifted sugar on the slab, and use it to line very small tartlet pans (previously slightly buttered), dry them in moderate heat of a light-fawn color, fill them to within the eighth of an inch of the edge with red-currant jelly, dry them again for ten minutes in the screen, and then mask them over with rose-pink transparent icing.

BONBON TARTLETS, WHITE.

Prepare the tartlets as in the foregoing, fill them with apple jelly, and *glacez* them over with transparent icing.

BONBON TARTLETS WITH CHOCOLATE.

These are to be filled with damson jam or apricot marmalade, and *glacés* with transparent chocolate-icing.

BONBON TARTLETS WITH GREENGAGE.

Fill the tartlets prepared with almond-paste, and ice or *glacez* them over with transparent green icing.

BONBON TARTLETS WITH APRICOT JAM.

Fill the tartlets, prepared as before, with bright apricot jam, and *glacez* them over with transparent icing.

BONBON ALMOND-PASTE ROUT-CAKES.

Prepare the paste as described for ornamental rout-cakes, roll it out rather thin, cut it up or stamp it out with small tin cutters of about the size of half-crown pieces, bake these on buttered baking-plates (moderate heat) of light color; when done, stick two of the pieces together with some kind of jam, mask their surfaces with similar jam, and *glacez* them with any kind of transparent icing described in this work.

CHAPTER IX.

BOUCHÉES, OR DESSERT-CAKES, GLACÉS WITH WHOLE FRUITS
AND PRESERVES.

GENERAL REMARKS. — BOUCHÉES DE DAMES. — BOUCHÉES WITH APRI-
COTS. — BOUCHÉES WITH GREEN APRICOTS. — BOUCHÉES WITH PINE-
APPLE. — BOUCHÉES WITH CHERRIES. — BOUCHÉES WITH GREENGAGES.
— BOUCHÉES WITH PEACHES. — BOUCHÉES WITH ORANGES. — BOUCHÉES
GARNISHED WITH PRESERVE.

GENERAL REMARKS.

THIS kind of dessert-cake has a most elegant aspect, and is, moreover, a most delicious morsel, and contributes in a great degree to render the dessert both elegant and *recherché*. Great care should be exercised in trimming the cakes of even shapes before attempting to finish them; and for this purpose a tin cutter should be used to stamp off any uneven asperities that may present themselves round their edges.

BOUCHÉES DE DAMES.

Prepare some sponge or cup cake batter; lay this out by pushing it through a biscuit-forcer, in rounds measuring one inch and a half in diameter, upon a sheet of paper spread on a baking-sheet, dredge some sugar over their surfaces, and bake them of a light color; and when done, trimmed, and placed upon a wire drainer, place a circular piece of red-currant jelly, or any other preserve, on the tops, and gloss or *glacez* them over with transparent icing. After they have been set to dry in the screen for a bare ten minutes, they will be ready.

NOTE. — These, and all other *bouchées* described in this chapter, are intended to be used for *dressing* what are termed *tambours*, or dessert-drums ; that is, certain ornaments forming part of a dessert-service, which are constructed so as to present two, and sometimes three, graduated kinds of shelves, upon which these and similar cakes are to be placed in rows.

BOUCHÉES WITH APRICOTS.

With some rich cake-batter prepare some round drops, as shown in the preceding case ; and when done, trimmed, and placed on a wire drainer, place the half of a preserved apricot upon each *bouchée,* and allow any excess of moisture from the syrup to become entirely absorbed into the cake before you attempt to gloss or *glacer* them with transparent noyeau-icing. When finished, dry them for a few minutes in the screen.

BOUCHÉES WITH GREEN APRICOTS.

Prepare these in a similar manner to the foregoing, excepting that green apricots must be used in this instance : these must be divided in halves, and placed upon the *bouchées* so as to form a kind of star, and are to be glossed over with transparent icing flavored with cedrati liqueur.

BOUCHÉES WITH PINE-APPLE.

Prepare some small round cake-drops about one inch and a half in diameter ; place rather smaller slices of thin preserved pine-apple upon each of these, and gloss or *glacez* them over with transparent icing flavored with pine-apple syrup.

BOUCHÉES WITH CHERRIES.

Prepare the cake-drops as before, place some preserved cherries upon them, and gloss or *glacez* them over with transparent icing flavored with kirschenwasser.

BOUCHÉES WITH GREENGAGES.

Prepare the cake-drops, place the halves of greengages preserved in syrup upon them, and gloss or *glacez* them over with transparent icing flavored with maraschino.

BOUCHÉES WITH PEACHES.

Proceed as in the foregoing cases, and gloss them over with transparent icing flavored with noyeau and tinged with carmine.

BOUCHÉES WITH ORANGES.

Place thin slices of oranges done in a little syrup upon the *bouchées*, and gloss them over with transparent icing: flavor them with zest of orange or with Curaçoa liqueur.

BOUCHÉES GARNISHED WITH PRESERVE.

Use any kind of marmalade or preserve to stick two of the drops together, and gloss or *glacez* their surfaces with any kind of tranparent icing.

CHAPTER X.

ICE CREAMS.

GENERAL DIRECTIONS. — LEMON OR VANILLA ICE CREAM. — CHOCOLATE CREAM ICE. — FLOWING ICED PUNCH. — MARASCHINO ICE CREAM. — PINE-APPLE CREAM ICE. — ORANGE CREAM ICE. — GINGER CREAM ICE. — ITALIAN CREAM ICE. — PISTACHIO CREAM ICE. — ORANGE-FLOWER CREAM ICE. — NOUGAT CREAM ICE. — LIQUEUR CREAM ICE. — BOURBON CREAM ICE. — CHESTERFIELD CREAM ICE. — WHOLE-RICE CREAM ICE. — STRAWBERRY CREAM ICE. — RASPBERRY CREAM ICE. — APRICOT CREAM ICE. — PEACH CREAM ICE. — CHERRY CREAM ICE.

GENERAL REMARKS.

FOR making the best ice cream, use rich sweet cream sweetened with finely powdered sugar, and flavor with the extracts of vanilla, lemon, &c., to be procured of first-class druggists. This will be found more convenient than any other mode of flavoring. If preferred, however, the vanilla-bean may be used by boiling in sweet milk until the aroma is obtained, then strained, and, when cool, added to the sweetened cream. In all cases, avoid setting the cream near the fire if the weather is warm, as it will not bear any heat without danger of turning sour, and should be kept in the milk-cellar or refrigerator until time to prepare it for freezing.

When cream cannot be had, an excellent substitute may be provided as follows: To a quart of new milk add two beaten eggs; set it on the fire in a saucepan, but be careful not to stir it after it is hot, as that would be apt to make it burn. While it is heating, mix smoothly with a teacup of new milk a tablespoonful of flour, and be ready to stir it into the milk on the fire just as it comes to the boiling point. Remove it immediately, and pour it into another vessel to cool. This is known to cooks as boiled custard; and although some take more than two eggs, that number, used as directed, will be found sufficient to make a delicious substitute for cream, and, for this purpose, all the more desirable because not tasting so much of the egg, the color also being that of a very rich cream. The custard thus prepared should now be sweetened well, and treated just as in making with cream, with the exception that this requires the addition of a small pinch of salt; and, when the whole is frozen, very few can distinguish it from genuine ice cream; indeed, half of that sold in confectionery establishments is prepared in the above way. Some confectioners use arrowroot instead of flour for thickening; but either the latter or corn-starch is better for the purpose, as they have less taste of their own.

FREEZING. — Within a few years, much improvement has been made in the apparatus for freezing ices. Formerly the cream was placed in simple tin freezers, and, as the ice formed around the sides, it was scraped off by spoons into the centre, the operation being constantly repeated until the whole became thick. Of course this was a slow process, and the constant removal of the lid (which was unavoidable), besides being very tiresome, had many other disadvantages; while the plan of scraping and stirring in the ice, after hours of labor, produced, generally, a very rough and inferior article.

By the modern method, the freezer is a cylindrical tin vessel, which is provided with a rotary scraper or dasher moving by a crank, with handle coming through the lid. The cream or custard is prepared, and then placed in this freezer, which must be firmly embedded in a bucket of pounded ice mixed with coarse salt.* This bucket should be provided with a hole or spigot near the bottom, so as to drain off the superfluous water caused by the melting ice. The lid of the freezer must be tight-fitting and secure, so as to avoid all danger of the salt getting into it. As soon as the freezer is firmly fixed, and entirely surrounded with the compound of salt and ice, commence turning the handle, and continue to turn until it is well frozen, which is soon indicated by the increased difficulty of moving the crank. As soon as it becomes stiff, the lid may be lifted and the dasher removed (they are usually movable), using a spoon to scrape off the cream which adheres to it. If it is to be moulded, the tin forms may now be filled. If a pyramid is used, put a spoonful of the softest frozen cream into the extreme point, being careful that it fills up well; then go on filling it up, pressing the frozen cream into every part. Some force is required to pack tightly, in order to give firmness and body to the form when removed from the mould. When entirely full, put the lid securely on the mould, and plunge it into a bed of salted ice, there to remain until time for serving. When about to serve, have ready a plate with a flat bottom somewhat larger than the base of the pyramid, also a pan of hot water; roll the tin form, for an instant only, in the water, then wipe quickly, and, holding it top downwards, remove the lid, place the plate over it, and quickly turn it right side up, setting the plate on the table; remove the tin mould carefully, and the pyramid will remain standing on the plate. Another plan is to wipe the outside of the mould on taking it from the ice-bed; then take off the lid, and set the pyramid, base downwards, on the plate; wring cloths out of scalding water, and wrap them around the tin mould for a few minutes until the cream is sufficiently melted to allow the tin to be lifted off.

LEMON OR VANILLA ICE CREAM.

Proceed as directed above, using either the vanilla-bean bruised and boiled in a little milk, or the grated rinds of good lemons; or, if more convenient, the extracts of lemon or vanilla, to be had of druggists. Flavor and sweeten according to taste.

CHOCOLATE CREAM ICE.

Boil one quart of milk; grate half a pound of best French chocolate, and stir into the milk; let it boil until thick: add a quarter of a pound of sugar. When cool, add one quart of cream: stir well, and pour into the freezer.

ANOTHER CHOCOLATE CREAM ICE.

Ingredients: 8 oz. of chocolate, 12 oz. of sugar, a pint of water, 8 yolks of eggs, a tablespoonful of strong vanilla-sugar, and a pint of double cream whipped.

First dissolve the chocolate with the water by either placing it at the entrance of the oven or near the fire, and afterwards whisking it to render it smooth; then mix it with the yolk of eggs, sugar, and vanilla; stir the composition on the fire to set it; strain, freeze the ice, and finish by adding the whipped cream.

FLOWING ICED PUNCH.

Ingredients: juice of 36 lemons, 5 lbs. sugar, 2 qts. champagne, 2 qts. cream, ¼ oz. tea, 2 qts. water.

First boil the sugar with one quart of water; then put in the lemon-juice, with the grated peel of eight lemons; boil the tea with one pint of water, strain through a sieve, and freeze it all in a large box that could hold four quarts more than what has been put in; add the champagne, little by little, when it has frozen hard; then add the cream: take it out, and stand it in champagne glasses.

MARASCHINO ICE CREAM.

Ingredients: cream, 1 qt.; sugar, ⅔ lb.; maraschino to taste. Mix well together, and freeze. In this way can be made ices flavored with various liqueurs.

PINE-APPLE CREAM ICE.

Ingredients: 1 lb. of pine-apple pulp, made by peeling, grating, cutting up small, or pounding and rubbing the pulp through a strainer; 12 oz. of sugar, 1½ pint of milk or cream, and 3 yolks of eggs.

Mix these ingredients in a stewpan, and stir all together on the fire to thicken the cream without allowing it to come to the boil at all; rub the composition through a sieve or strainer into a dish, and afterwards pour it into a basin previously to its being iced or frozen.

ORANGE CREAM ICE.

Ingredients: 1½ pt. of milk or cream, 12 oz. of sugar, the rind of 2 oranges rubbed on sugar, the juice of 6 oranges, 3 yolks of eggs.

Mix the ingredients in a stewpan, and stir them over the fire until the composition begins to thicken; work all together briskly, and rub or pass the cream through a strainer. Freeze the ice in the usual way.

GINGER CREAM ICE.

Ingredients: 1½ pt. of milk or cream, 12 oz. of sugar, 6 oz. of preserved ginger cut small, 3 yolks of eggs.

Set the composition by stirring it over the fire until it begins to thicken, and, when cold, freeze it in the usual manner.

ITALIAN CREAM ICE.

Ingredients: 1½ pt. of milk or cream, 3 yolks of eggs, 12 oz. of sugar, 6 oz. of prâlines or burnt almonds bruised to a smooth pulp, 3 cloves, a bit of cinnamon and 12 coriander seeds bruised, the rind of 2 oranges, a gill of cognac brandy, and 6 oz. of candied orange, lemon, and citron peels in equal proportions.

Mix the milk, sugar, yolks of eggs, prâlines pulp, spices,

and rind all together in a stewpan, and stir the composition on the fire until it thickens; then rub it through a strainer into a basin.

The candied peels will have been cut in small squares, and soaked in the brandy, ready to be added to the composition previously to its being set up in the freezer. Finish the ice in the usual manner.

PISTACHIO CREAM ICE.

Ingredients: 1½ pt. of milk or cream, 12 oz. of sugar, 6 oz. of scalded cleaned pistachios pulverized into a pulp, 3 yolks of eggs, a tablespoonful of orange-flower water, and two tablespoonfuls of spinach greening.

Mix the whole of the ingredients, with the exception of the greening and the flavoring, in a stewpan, and stir all together on the fire to set or thicken the composition; then rub this through a strainer into a basin, and afterwards mix in the flavoring and greening perfectly smooth. Some of the cream must first be worked up with the greening, otherwise the coloring would prove unsatisfactory, as it would be imperfectly mixed. Set up and freeze the ice as directed.

ORANGE-FLOWER CREAM ICE.

Ingredients: 1½ pt. of milk or cream, 12 oz. of sugar, 1 oz. of candied orange-flowers, 3 yolks of eggs.

Bruise the orange-flowers, mix and stir the whole of the ingredients on the fire until the composition begins to thicken; then strain it into a basin. Freeze and finish the ice in the usual manner.

NOUGAT CREAM ICE.

It is customary to make this kind of ice when it happens that some nougat is left from a previous preparation, although there is no reason why it should not be purposely prepared for the occasion. Bruise the nougat in the mortar with half a gill of orange-flower water; add this to 8 yolks of eggs, 12 oz. of sugar, 1½ pt. of single cream, and 3 drops of essence of peach-kernels; stir the composition on the fire, and, as soon as it begins to thicken, rub it through a strainer into a basin. When cooled, freeze the ice in the usual way.

LIQUEUR CREAM ICE.

Ingredients: 1½ pt. of double cream whipped, 12 oz. of sifted sugar, and a gill of any kind of liqueur.

Mix, freeze, and set the ice up in its mould.

LIQUEUR CREAM ICE, ANOTHER WAY.

Ingredients: 1½ pt. of milk, 12 oz. of sugar, 8 yolks of eggs, and a gill of any kind of liqueur.

Mix the milk, eggs, and sugar; set the composition over the fire, strain it, add the liqueur, freeze the ice, and set it up in its mould.

BOURBON CREAM ICE.

Ingredients: a custard made with 1 pt. of milk, 12 oz. of sugar, and 3 yolks of eggs; ½ pt. of milk of almonds made with 6 oz. of sweet almonds and 12 bitter almonds; 2 oz. of currants, 2 oz. of candied orange-peel, 2 oz. of candied citron-peel, 2 oz. of dried cherries, 2 oz. of cut pine-apple, a few drops of vanilla essence, and a gill of maraschino.

Soak the fruits in the maraschino, mix the custard with the milk of almonds and the vanilla; freeze this stiff; then add the fruits, work the ice again, and, when set quite firm, set it up in its mould.

CHESTERFIELD CREAM ICE.

Ingredients: a cinnamon and lemon custard composed of 1½ pt. of milk, 12 oz. of sugar, 3 yolks of eggs, a stick of cinnamon, the rind of a lemon, and a small compote of damsons with a little thick syrup.

Freeze the custard stiff, then add half a pint of double cream whipped; set up the ice in a plain mould with a hollowed smooth cavity in the centre, leaving one and a half inches thickness of the ice round the sides of the mould; nearly fill this hollow with the damsons, cover them in with more ice, put a lid on the mould, embed it in rough ice and salt, and, when sent to table, garnish the base with Chesterfield biscuits.

WHOLE-RICE CREAM ICE.

Ingredients: 1½ pt. of milk, 12 oz. of sugar, 3 yolks of eggs, 4 oz. of rice boiled soft in a pt. of milk and reduced to half that quantity, a gill of curaçoa, ½ pt. of milk of almonds, and a compote of 6 oranges.

Mix the cream, sugar, milk of almonds, and the yolks of eggs, and make these into a custard; add the liqueur and the boiled rice, freeze the composition, and set up the ice in its mould. When turned out on its dish, garnish round the base with the pieces of oranges, and pour the syrup over all.

STRAWBERRY CREAM ICE.

Ingredients: 1 pt. of double cream, 1 lb. of picked strawberries pressed through a coarse hair sieve, 12 oz. of sifted sugar, or, what would be better still, nearly a pint of syrup of 32 degrees strength, and a few drops of cochineal to increase the color if needed, as some strawberries are too pale to impart a sufficiently deep tinge when mixed with cream.

Mix the ingredients, freeze and work the composition to give the ice sufficient body, and set up the ice in its mould.

RASPBERRY CREAM ICE.

The same as strawberry.

APRICOT CREAM ICE.

Ingredients: 1 pt. of thick apricot pulp, prepared by peeling 12 apricots and boiling them with a gill of water until dissolved, stirring them while on the fire, and rubbing the pulp through a strainer; 1 pt. of thick syrup, 1 pt. of cream, and a few drops of essence of kernels.

Proceed as before directed.

PEACH CREAM ICE.

The same as apricots, using six ripe peaches for the purpose, and adding a few drops of cochineal to give a pink-blush tint to the composition.

CHERRY CREAM ICE.

Ingredients: 1½ lb. of red cherries, picked, pounded, boiled up with a gill of water in a copper pan, and rubbed through a hair sieve; 1 pint of thick syrup, 1 pint of cream, a few drops of cochineal, and a few drops of essence of kernels.

Mix the ingredients, freeze and work the ice, and mould it.

CHAPTER XI.

WATER AND FRUIT ICES.

FRUIT WATER ICE. — RED-CURRANT WATER ICE. — RASPBERRY WATER ICE. — STRAWBERRY WATER ICE. — CHERRY WATER ICE. — PINE-APPLE WATER ICE. — ORANGE WATER ICE. — LEMON WATER ICE. — PEACH WATER ICE. — APRICOT WATER ICE. — GREENGAGE WATER ICE. — DAMSON WATER ICE. — POMEGRANATE WATER ICE. — BARBERRY WATER ICE. — TUTTIFRUTTI OR MACEDOINE WATER ICE.

FRUIT WATER ICE.

IN preparing water ices, the chief rule is to be careful of the amount of flavoring and sweetening used. The tendency of the freezing process is to destroy the flavor, or, at least, to extract it; so that, in sweetening the mixture, it is best to make it rather sweeter than nceessary for use without freezing. In the following receipts for preparing fruit ices, directions are generally given to strain the mixture so as to exclude particles of fruit or pulp; some, however, prefer it to be retained, with the pieces of fruit congealed here and there among the ice : of course, every one can decide this question according to his own taste, either way being very palatable. The use of syrup of different degrees of strength is recommended as the best and simplest method for amalgamation with and giving body to the other ingredients composing the ices : in many cases, however, it will be quite sufficient to use the refined powdered sugar without any previous preparation.

In moulding fruit ices, soufflés, and other small preparations, it is often necessary to have the benefit of a freezing temperature, without its being either proper or practicable to plunge the articles into the bed of salted ice. For this purpose, a contrivance known as an ice-cave has been provided. They are usually of copper or tin, either round or square, and may be of from twelve to twenty-four inches in diameter, with a depth nearly as great, and a tightly-fitting lid made with sides so as to admit of ice being placed on top of the cave. A very good substitute, however, can be improvised with a tin kettle of sufficient depth and good lid. When this cave is buried in the ice-tub filled with powdered ice and salt, its contents will become nicely frozen, and can be kept hardened for any required time.

RED-CURRANT WATER ICE.

Ingredients: 1 pt. of syrup of 32 degrees strength, 1½ pt. of juice made by pressing and straining two-thirds of red currants picked, and one-third of raspberries; the fruit must be in sufficient quantity to produce the 1½ pt. of juice, say 1½ lb. of currants, and 8 oz. of raspberries, and a gill of water.

There is a second method for extracting the juice of currants, and other similar fruits, which consists in placing the above-named quantities, with rather better than a gill of water, in a copper pan, just giving them a few minutes' simmering on the fire, and afterwards pressing out the juice through a cloth by wringing it.

Process: mix the currant-juice and the syrup in a basin, and use the saccharometer, or syrup-gauge, to ascertain that the composition, in order to be in accordance with the required strength, marks 24 degrees. In the event of the composition being too thin, — too poor in sugar, — the saccharometer would mark below the 24 degrees; and this will be rectified by adding a little more syrup to bring the composition to the right point. If too rich in sugar, it will then mark a higher number than 24: add a little water to establish the correct proportions by reducing it to 24 degrees.

Proceed with the freezing as before directed.

RASPBERRY WATER ICE.

Ingredients: 1½ pt. of raspberry-juice, made by pressing the fruit upon a hair sieve, or else using the fruit-presser; 1 pt. of 32 degrees syrup, a glass of currant-juice, or the juice of half a lemon.

For freezing and setting up the ice, proceed as before directed.

STRAWBERRY WATER ICE.

Ingredients: 1¼ pt. of strawberry juice or pulp, made by pressing 1½ lbs. of picked strawberries, with a wooden spoon, through a strainer; 1 pt. of 32 degrees syrup, the juice of half a lemon, a few drops of cochineal, and a gill of water.

Mix the ingredients; work the composition in the freezer, and, when sufficiently frozen, set up the ice in its mould.

The addition of one white of egg of Italian meringue-paste, in finishing this or any other fruit water ice, constitutes the Neapolitan method of ice-making. The meringue gives a greater body to the composition, and also renders an ice more unctuous.

CHERRY WATER ICE.

Ingredients: 1¼ pt. of cherry-juice, made by pressing 2 lbs. of red cherries, with a wooden spoon, upon and through a strainer to extract their juice, and pouring a gill of spring water over the dregs to avoid wasting any portion of the fruit; a pt. of 32 degrees syrup, a few drops of cochineal, the juice of a lemon, and two drops of essence of kernels.

Proceed as in the foregoing case.

PINE-APPLE WATER ICE.

Ingredients: 1 lb. of pine-apple, peeled, sliced, reduced into a pulp by pounding, it and rubbed through a strainer (wash the dregs with half a pint of spring water); 1 pt. of syrup, and the juice of a lemon.

Proceed as before.

ORANGE WATER ICE.

Ingredients: the juice of 12 oranges, the juice of 2 lemons, the thin rind of 3 oranges, infused in the warm syrup for an hour, and afterwards strained to the juice; 1 pt. of syrup.

Freeze the composition in the usual way, and set up the ice in its mould.

LEMON WATER ICE.

Ingredients: the juice of 10 lemons, the rind of 3, infused in a pint of warm syrup, and strained; 1 white of Italian meringue.

Mix and freeze the composition, and afterwards incorporate the meringue-paste by degrees.

PEACH WATER ICE.

Ingredients: 10 ripe peaches, sliced without peeling, boiled soft with half a pint of water, and rubbed through a strainer; 1 pint of syrup, the juice of a lemon, 3 drops of essence of kernels, and a pinch of carmine.

Mix and freeze the composition as usual.

APRICOT WATER ICE.

Ingredients: 18 ripe apricots *pulped* as above with half a pint of water, a pint of syrup, 3 drops of essence of kernels.

Finish the ice in the usual way.

GREENGAGE WATER ICE.

Ingredients: 2 dozen ripe greengages *pulped* by boiling them with half a pint of water, and afterwards rubbing them through a strainer; 1 pint of syrup, 3 drops of vanilla, a tablespoonful of spinach-greening.

First mix the pulp, by degrees, with the greening; then add the syrup and the vanilla. Freeze, and set up the ice in its mould.

DAMSON WATER ICE.

Ingredients: 1 qt. of damsons *pulped*, 1¼ pt. of syrup, 1 white of egg of Italian meringue-paste.

Proceed as in raspberry water ice.

POMEGRANATE WATER ICE.

Ingredients: the pips of 6 or 8 ripe pomegranates pressed, with a wooden spoon, through a strainer, to produce a pint of juice; 1 pint of syrup, a few drops of essence of vanilla, a few drops of cochineal, the juice of a lemon.

Proceed as before.

BARBERRY WATER ICE.

Ingredients: 2 lbs. of ripe barberries boiled with a gill of water in a sugar-boiler and pressed through a strainer, 1 pint of thick syrup, a few drops of vanilla, a few drops of cochineal.

Mix the juice, syrup, vanilla, and the cochineal; freeze the composition; incorporate the whole; freeze again, and mould the ice.

TUTTIFRUTTI, OR MACEDOINE ICE.

Ingredients: 1 pt. of syrup, 1 gill of kirschenwasser, a few drops of vanilla, the juice of 3 lemons, a macedoine composed of a pint of fruits in the following proportions, — of cherries stoned, pine-apple cut small, strawberries, grapes, candied peels, apricots, peaches, all cut small, equal proportions, to form the quantity required.

Mix the syrup, liqueur, vanilla, and lemon-juice; freeze the composition; add the macedoine of fruits, mix lightly, and mould the ice.

CHAPTER XII.

IMITATION SOUFFLÉS ICED, AND BISCUITS ICED.

IMITATION SOUFFLÉ ICED À LA LONDONDERRY. — SOUFFLÉ ICED À LA WALTER SCOTT. — SOUFFLÉ ICED À LA BYRON. — SOUFFLÉ ICED À LA CHARLES KEAN. — ICED BISCUITS À LA CHARLES DICKENS. — ICED BISCUITS À LA THACKERAY.

IMITATION SOUFFLÉ ICED À LA LONDONDERRY.

INGREDIENTS : 1 pt. of syrup of 32 degrees strength, 15 yolks of eggs, ½ pt. of filtered strawberry-juice, ½ pt. of maraschino, a pinch of salt, 3 gills of double cream whipped.

Mix the syrup with the yolks of eggs; then strain it into a copper egg-bowl previously warmed with *hot* water and wiped out; add the liqueur, strawberry-juice, and salt, and lightly yet briskly whisk the composition (with the bottom of the bowl standing six inches deep in hot water) till it assumes the appearance of a substantial creamy batter, and at the same time begins to feel tepid to the touch: you will continue whisking the composition for about ten minutes longer out of the water; then, the *soufflé*-case being already placed in the ice-cave, lightly and gently incorporate the whipped cream, and pour the composition into the case, which must have a wide band of cartridge-paper pinned closely round it, the band to be of sufficient width to admit of its rising one inch and a half above the edge of the case, so that when the band is withdrawn, previously to sending the *soufflé* to table, it may have the appearance of having risen out of the case like an ordinary *soufflé*.

Iced Biscuits. 79

IMITATION SOUFFLÉ ICED À LA WALTER SCOTT.

Ingredients: 1 pt. of syrup of 32 degrees strength, 15 yolks of eggs, a gill of curaçoa, ½ a gill of orange-flower water, ½ a gill of juice of oranges, ½ a pt. of double cream whipped.

Proceed as before.

IMITATION SOUFFLÉ ICED À LA BYRON.

Ingredients: 1 pt. of syrup of 32 degrees strength, ½ pt. of noyeau, ½ pt. of juice of cherries, 2 oz. of bruised macaroons, ½ pt. of double cream whipped.

Proceed as in preceding.

IMITATION SOUFFLÉ ICED À LA CHARLES KEAN.

Ingredients: 1 pt. of syrup of 32 degrees strength, 3 gills of filtered raspberry-juice, the juice of 1 lemon, a gill of maraschino, 15 yolks, 2 oz. of chocolate drops, and ½ pt. of double cream whipped.

Mix the syrup and yolks of eggs, and strain this into the warmed egg-bowl, then add the raspberry and lemon juices and the liqueur; whisk the composition till it creams substantially, then whisk it off the hot water for ten minutes longer, add the chocolate-drops and the whipped cream; lightly fill the case, set it in the cave placed in a tub well buried in pounded rough ice with salt, and, two hours after, take it out, remove the band of paper from round the case, cover the surface of the *soufflé* with powdered baked savoy biscuit, and serve immediately.

ICED BISCUITS À LA CHARLES DICKENS.

Ingredients: 1 pt. of syrup of 32 degrees strength, 15 yolks of eggs, 3 gills of peach-pulp pinked with carmine, 1 gill of noyeau, ½ pint of double cream whipped, and a small quantity of chocolate water ice made with ½ pt. of syrup, with 4 oz. of best chocolate very smoothly dissolved in it, and frozen, ready to be used as hereinafter indicated.

Mix the syrup and yolks of eggs (strained) with the peach-pulp and the noyeau and a few drops of essence of vanilla, and whisk the composition as directed previously: when ready for freezing, pour this into brick-shaped moulds, and set these embedded in rough ice with salt to be refrozen for an hour and a half; at the end of that time, they are to be unmoulded, cut up into slices an inch thick, coated all over, or, at all events, on the upper surface and sides, with the ready frozen chocolate ice, smoothed with a knife dipped in cold water, placed in an ice-cave: as soon as the cave is filled with the biscuits, let it be entirely buried in rough ice with salt. An hour and a half afterwards, they will be ready for table.

These biscuits may be dished up with leaf-shaped pieces of green preserved angelica, or placed in small oblong-shaped white paper cases made to their size.

ICED BISCUITS À LA THACKERAY.

Ingredients: 1 pt. of syrup of 32 degrees strength, 1 pt. of strawberry-pulp, 15 yolks of eggs, 1 oz. of vanilla-sugar, ½ pt. of double cream whipped.

Mix the syrup and yolks, strain, then add the strawberry pulp and vanilla-sugar, set the composition as directed first; incorporate the whipped cream lightly, and fill the paper cases (either plated and circular, or square). These must be surrounded each with a band of stiff paper of sufficient width to reach half an inch above the edges of the cases, the bands to be pinched, stuck, or pinned together at one corner, so as to render them secure. The biscuits filled, place them in the ice-cave, and embed this in ice in the usual way.

When about to send these biscuits to table, after having first removed the bands of paper, cover their surfaces with brown-colored ratafias bruised to a fine powder and sifted upon them. It will be obvious that the bands of paper to be placed round the cases are intended to give the biscuits the appearance of the composition having risen out of the cases, while the biscuits are supposed to have been baked.

CHAPTER XIII.

ICED PUDDINGS.

ICED PUDDING À LA PERCY BYSSHE SHELLEY.—ICED PUDDING À LA SHAKSPEARE.—ICED PUDDING À LA VICTORIA.—ICED PUDDING À LA KEMBLE.

ICED PUDDING A LA PERCY BYSSHE SHELLEY.

INGREDIENTS: a custard cream composed of 6 yolks of eggs, a pint of cream, 12 oz. of sugar, and 1 oz. of vanilla-sugar; 6 oz. of fruits consisting of equal parts of dried cherries, pine-apple, dried pears, and green citron, all cut in very small squares; and a gill of maraschino.

Mix the custard and the maraschino, and freeze the composition quite stiff; then add the fruits, freeze again, fill the mould, embed it in rough ice and salt.

ICED PUDDING À LA SHAKSPEARE.

Ingredients: a custard cream composed of 1 pt. of cream, 8 yolks of eggs, and 8 oz. of sugar; $\frac{1}{2}$ a pt. of caramel composed of 4 oz. of sugar, a stick of cinnamon, the rind of a lemon, and a gill of water, boiled down and baked of a very dark brown color, and diluted with $\frac{1}{2}$ a pint of water, and strained; a gill of curaçoa, 8 oz. of dried fruits as follows,— candied orange-peel, shred pistachios, dried pears, and pine-apple, in equal parts, and all cut small; 3 gills of double cream whipped.

Mix the custard, the essence of caramel, and the liqueurs; freeze the composition; add the shreds of fruits and the whipped cream; mould the ice, and embed it in rough ice and salt in the usual way.

Iced Puddings.

ICED PUDDING À LA VICTORIA.

Ingredients: 1½ pt. of custard ice, 4 oz. of dried apricots cut small, 4 oz. of dried cherries, 2 oz. of Diavolini, ½ pt. of double cream whipped.

Freeze the custard quite stiff; then add the fruits and the whipped cream, and mould the ice. When turned out of the mould (melon-shaped), the exterior of the pudding must be sprinkled over with chopped almonds dried of a light-brown color, and chopped pistachios: these are intended to have the rugged appearance of the peel of the melon.

The top and base of the pudding should be garnished with small fancy fruit-shaped ices.

ICED PUDDING À LA CHARLES KEMBLE.

Ingredients: a custard cream composed of 1 pt. of cream, 8 yolks of eggs, ½ pt. of pine-apple syrup, 8 oz. of sugar, 6 oz. of corn-farina, and 1 oz. of vanilla-sugar, 4 oz. of pine-apple cut small, 4 oz. of Sultana raisins, a gill of kirschenwasser, and ½ pt. of double cream whipped.

Mix the custard and liqueur, freeze the composition, add the fruit and the whipped cream, and mould the ice.

These iced puddings may be further varied by using other receipts for cream ices given before.

CHAPTER XIV

ICED BEVERAGES CALLED GRANITI.

GENERAL INSTRUCTIONS. — ORGEAT, OR MILK OF ALMONDS. — COFFEE GRANITO. — ANOTHER METHOD OF FREEZING GRANITI. — CLARET GRANITO. — SHERRY GRANITO. — PUNCH GRANITO. — FRUIT-JUICE GRANITO.

INSTRUCTIONS FOR THE PREPARATION OF ICED BEVERAGES CALLED GRANITI.

THESE beverages are considered most deliciously grateful drinks at evening parties in the summer season. They are chiefly composed of fruit juices and syrup: they are also made with different kinds of punch, and the coffee granito is a special favorite with all connoisseurs. Graniti of all descriptions, more particularly those composed of lemonade, orangeade, orgeat, and coffee, are especially in great request in Italy.

ORGEAT, OR MILK OF ALMONDS.

Scald six ounces of Jordan almonds and one ounce of bitter almonds; remove the skins, and soak the almonds in cold water for several hours; then pound them thoroughly into a pulp with half a gill of orange-flower water, and put this into an earthen pan with eight ounces of the finest loaf-sugar and three pints of spring-water; stir well together, cover the pan over, and, at the end of an hour, strain through a clear sieve. The pan must be kept on the ice. Iced water is added for use.

COFFEE GRANITO.

Ingredients: 1 pt. of strong bright coffee, ½ pt. of syrup of 28 degrees strength.

Mix the coffee and syrup in a freezer; twirl the composition first to the right, and then to the left, and, as it becomes frozen up the sides of the freezer, detach it by scraping it down into the centre with the spatula; bearing in mind that granito must be only half frozen, so as to resemble snowy-like water, just sufficiently liquid to admit of its being poured into glasses to be handed round to the guests.

ANOTHER METHOD OF FREEZING GRANITI.

The composition should be put into water-bottles or jugs; twirled round in the ice; and, as the contents become frozen up the interior of the bottles, a narrow wooden spatula should be thrust in for the purpose of scraping down the frozen portion into the liquid. When graniti are frozen in perfection, the minute particles of the frozen portion of the composition resemble a numerous constellation of small crystals.

CLARET GRANITO.

To one quart of orangeade add a bottle of claret, and freeze as above.

SHERRY GRANITO.

To one quart of lemonade add a bottle of sherry, and freeze.

PUNCH GRANITO.

To one quart of any of the clear punches contained herein add one and a half pints of spring-water; freeze.

FRUIT-JUICE GRANITO.

All kinds of summer beverages contained in this may be appropriately used for the preparation of granito. For the method of freezing them, directions have been already given.

CHAPTER XV

DIFFERENT KINDS OF ICED PUNCH.

GIN PUNCH. — RUM PUNCH. — REGENT PUNCH. — BISHOP. — HEIDELBERG BISHOP. — PRINCE-OF-WALES PUNCH. — CHESTERFIELD PUNCH. — BEAUFORT PUNCH. — ROMAN PUNCH. — ROMAN PUNCH À LA MONTROSE. —

GIN PUNCH.

To half a pint of genuine old gin add one gill of maraschino, the juice of two lemons, the rind of one (previously infused in the gin), one and a half gill of strong syrup, and a quart bottle of seltzer-water. Ice the punch for one hour.

RUM PUNCH.

Put the following ingredients into a stone pitcher capable of holding a couple of gallons : 1 qt. of brandy, 1 qt. of rum, ½ pt. of old rack, ½ pt. of strong-made green tea, the juice of 12 lemons, the thin rind of 4, 1 small nutmeg grated, a good stick of cinnamon well bruised, 12 cloves bruised, 30 coriander-seeds bruised, 2 lbs. of pine-apple cut in very thin slices, 2 lbs. of lump-sugar. Pour 2 qts. of boiling water to this, stir all together, tie a bladder over the top of the pitcher, and set it aside under lock and key to allow the ingredients to steep *undisturbed* for a couple of days. At the end of that time, boil two quarts of *sweet* genuine milk ; add this to the other ingredients, mix thoroughly, and, an hour afterwards, filter the punch through a *clean* beaver jelly-bag. When filtered, bottle off the punch, cork down tight, and keep the bottles in a good cellar. When required for use, ✽ let it be well iced.

REGENT PUNCH.

Put the following ingredients into a freezing-pot ready embedded in ice ; viz., 3 gills of syrup, 3 gills of pine-apple syrup, 1 pt. of brandy, 1 pt. of old rum, 1 gill of kirschen wasser, 1 gill of lemon-juice, a small teacupful of green tea, *not* strong, and a bottle of *genuine* champagne. The rind of a Seville orange should be steeped in the syrup previously to using it.

Mix, and half freeze the punch similarly to sorbet or granito.

NOTE.— This and several of the following kinds of punch are far better adapted to follow turtle-soup than Roman punch, from the fact that they are not so cloying.

BISHOP.

To one bottle of red French wine add two ounces of lump-sugar, the thin rind of an orange or a lemon, and six cloves ; make the bishop hot without allowing it to boil, and strain through a silver wine-strainer into a jug.

HEIDELBERG BISHOP.

To a bottle of red Rhenish wine add two ounces of lump-sugar, the rind of half a lemon, six coriander-seeds, a small stick of cinnamon, and a wine-glassful of kirschenwasser ; warm the bishop without boiling.

PRINCE-OF-WALES PUNCH.

Place the following ingredients in a freezing-pot ready embedded in rough ice ; viz., a bottle of sparkling Aï, a gill of maraschino, half a pint of thin bright strawberry-syrup, the juice of six oranges, the rind of one rubbed on sugar and scraped off into the mixture, and a pint-bottle of German seltzer-water. Ice the punch similarly to granito.

CHESTERFIELD PUNCH.

Place the following ingredients in a freezing-pot ready embedded in ice; viz., two bottles of champagne, half a pint of pine-apple syrup, half a pint of strawberry syrup, the juice of three oranges and of three lemons, the rind of one lemon rubbed on sugar, and a quart bottle of German seltzer-water. Ice well.

BEAUFORT PUNCH.

Place the following ingredients in a freezing-pot ready embedded in ice; viz., two bottles of high Sauterne, half a gill of curaçoa, the juice of four oranges, half a pint of pine-apple syrup, a quart-bottle of German seltzer-water, and an infusion composed as follows, — a bunch of fresh-gathered balm, ditto of burrage, six leaves of verbena, half a green hothouse-cucumber sliced thin; put all these to infuse in half a pint of very thin *cold* syrup for two hours. The above infusion is to be strained to the other ingredients. The punch must be well iced for about half an hour.

ROMAN PUNCH.

Place the following ingredients in a freezing-pot ready embedded in ice; viz., a quart of prepared lemon ice, a bottle of pink, or champagne rosé, a gill of maraschino, and a few drops of essence of vanilla; freeze the mixture, working it thoroughly with the spatula. The punch must be vigorously worked while adding the meringue by degrees: if you find that it is too stiff, add a little more champagne to liquefy it to the proper degree.

ROMAN PUNCH À LA MONTROSE.

Place the following ingredients in a freezing-pot embedded in rough ice; viz., a quart of cherry-water ice, a bottle of Moselle, a gill of kirschenwasser, and half a gill of noyeau. Work these ingredients thoroughly while freezing them.

CHAPTER XVI.

COFFEE.

HISTORY OF THE PLANT. — QUALITIES OF COFFEE. — MOCHA. — CAYENNE COFFEE. — BOURBON COFFEE. — MARTINIQUE COFFEE. — ST. DOMINGO COFFEE. — JAVA COFFEE. — CEYLON COFFEE. — ON ROASTING COFFEE. — COFFEE AS A BEVERAGE.

THIS precious seed is derived from the coffee-tree, *Coffea arabica* (Linn). The tree came originally from Arabia, and especially from Yeman, near Mocha. It grows to the height of about twenty feet; its branches grow opposite to each other, are knotted, and of a grayish tint; the leaves are oval, pointed towards the extremity, shining, and furnished with stipules. The coffee-tree is an evergreen: the flowers are white, growing in clusters from the axilla of the upper leaves. The fruit is a species of berry, not unlike the cherry. When ripe, it becomes of a somewhat blackish color, and contains a yellow pulp in which are the seeds which make COFFEE. They are perfectly hard, and two are found in each berry. The inner side is flat, and marked by a small longitudinal groove, while the outer side is convex.

The coffee-tree flowers in spring and fall, and the berries remain on the trees for nearly four months before they have attained complete maturity. In order to separate the seeds from the pulp which surrounds them, they are allowed to ferment a little, and are then exposed to the sun. Some of the growers steep them in water previously. The coffee so obtained is considered of inferior quality: it is of a grayish hue, and is termed *steeped coffee*. The best method is to submit the berries to the action of a mill, which separates the pulp without touching the berry. This coffee is the most valued.

Having given this brief account of the tree itself, we will proceed to say something of the history of this most popular beverage.

There is a tradition in the East, that the use of coffee was first suggested to a Persian shepherd by observing that his goats were always particularly wakeful after browsing on a certain shrub (the coffee-tree). Curious to try the effect on himself, he first made a decoction of the leaves, and finally of the berries, and ascertained that the beverage thus obtained prevented him from sleeping, and had an extraordinarily exhilarating effect.

He communicated to his comrades this discovery of the effects of the coffee-berry; and from this small and insignificant beginning arose the present universal use of this delicious beverage.

But the most authentic account of the introduction of coffee is contained in an Arabian manuscript, the most ancient work on coffee, in which we read that *Schehabeddin ben*, an author of the ninth century of the Hegira, or the fifteenth century of the Christian era, attributes to Gemaleddin (called Dhabani by another writer), a mufti of Aden, a city of Arabia Felix (now in the possession of the British, and known as the Gibraltar of the Red Sea), the introduction of coffee as a beverage into that country. It is asserted there that Gemaleddin, having travelled in Persia, had seen coffee drunk there; and when, on returning to his own country, he happened to fall ill, he was desirous of trying on himself the medicinal effects of the berry. Success crowned his efforts; and, in his experiments, he discovered other properties, of curing headache, preventing drowsiness, &c. He immediately recommended the use of coffee to the dervises, that they might, by its means, more easily pass the night in prayer.

Soon afterwards it began to be employed by men of letters, and lawyers; and but a short time elapsed before it came into use among merchants, and even mechanics, especially when they were compelled to toil all night. Finally it came into general use in the city of Aden; whence, extending to the neighboring cities, it at length reached Mecca, where it was at first used only by the dervises, from motives of religion.

In Egypt also, it would appear that it was at first partaken of with certain religious sentiments. The devotees, who introduced it there, assembled on Monday and Friday evenings to enjoy it; and, during the time of handing it round and imbibing it, many prayers and religious ejaculations were uttered.

The inhabitants of Mecca became at length so fascinated with this beverage, that, without any motive of religious devotion or study, they drank it publicly in houses, which took, from the berry, the name of coffee-houses, where they passed their time merrily in amusements, play, &c. The use of coffee afterwards spread to many Arabian cities, especially to Medina, Grand Cairo, and among the dervises of the province of Yemen, who drank it with reverence in a large earthen cup received respectfully from the hands of their superiors. The devotees of Cairo imitated the dervises of Yemen.

Finally the most rigid Mohammedans began to disapprove of the use of coffee on account of the frequent irregularities arising from excess in it, which resembled those arising from wine. The government was compelled to restrict its use; but the prohibition excited so much murmuring, that, in the end, all were free to drink it as they pleased.

The beverage found its way successively into Syria, Damascus, and Aleppo, without encountering any opposition. In 1556, eleven years after its introduction at Aden, it was brought to Constantinople by two men, named Schems and

Hekin, who, coming, the one from Damascus, and the other from Aleppo, opened two coffee-houses in that city, both elegantly decorated, which were at first frequented by poets, writers, and other persons who went thither to pass away the time.

The imams began to complain loudly that the mosques were deserted because the whole community flocked to the coffee-houses. The dervises and other religious Turks murmured against this abuse, which they regarded as even more reprehensible than that of taking wine. To put an end to it, they presented a supplication to the mufti, condemning the drinking of coffee as contrary to the Koran. From that time, no one durst openly violate the ordinance: the coffee-houses were closed, and officers superintended the execution of the orders of the mufti. Yet habit is second nature: it had become so strong, and the use of coffee so pleasant, that, notwithstanding it was forbidden, every one continued to drink it at home. The government, perceiving that it could not eradicate the custom, then thought of deriving a profit from it, and permitted it to be sold, on payment of a certain duty, and to be drunk, provided it was done privately. By degrees, the laws were relaxed, the coffee-houses were re-opened; and a mufti, less scrupulous than his predecessors, declared that coffee had no connection with charcoal (as the former mufti had declared), and that the beverage was in no respect contrary to the laws of Mohammed.

The grand vizier, having obtained an especial authority over coffee, subjected it to a heavy duty. In general, every coffee-house keeper was to pay a sequin a day to the government; and they were not permitted to charge more than an asper a cup, a hundred and forty-three aspers making a sequin.

According to the translation of this Arabic manuscript by Mr. Galland, the coffee-houses were closed from the time of the war in Candia, as long as the Ottoman affairs remained in a critical condition, in order to put a stop to the political discussions which took place in them. Notwithstanding this, coffee was drunk as much as ever: it was sold publicly in the squares and principal streets, where it was prepared on small portable furnaces. The prohibition of coffee-houses was only in Constantinople: they were open in all the other towns and villages; and, even where forbidden, the sale continued to increase. Turks, Jews, Greeks, Armenians, every one, in short, drank it at least twice a day; until, at last, so universal became its use, that for a man to refuse it to his wife was a legal cause of divorce.

The Turks drink their coffee very strong and clear, and without sugar: occasionally they put in a pinch of anise or of cardamom, or perhaps a drop of essence of amber.

It is not easy to determine the period when the use of coffee extended from Constantinople to the western countries of Europe. It appears, however, that the Venetians were the first to adopt it. Pierre Della Valle, a Venetian, in a letter written from Constantinople in 1615, announced to one of his friends, that, on his return, he would bring him some coffee. M. Galland relates, according to M. Lacroix, that Thévenot, on his return from a voyage to the East, in 1657, brought to Paris some coffee, with which he treated his friends. Some Armenians who afterwards arrived there brought it into more general use; but it did not acquire great popularity until 1671, on the occasion of the embassy of Solyman Aga, ambassador of Mohammed IV. Coffee had been known in Marseilles, however, as early as 1644. It had been brought thither by a gentleman who had accompanied M. de Lahaye in his embassy to Constantinople. In 1660, several bales of it were brought from Egypt, and its use became more general. In 1671, the first coffee-house was opened. Two years before this, an Armenian, who had been unsuccessful in business in Paris, opened a coffee-house in London; though Anderson's "Chronological History of Commerce" gives 1652 as the date of its introduction into England, by a Turkey merchant named Daniel Edwards, who brought home with him a Greek servant named *Pasqua*, who understood the arts of roasting and preparing coffee. This man was the first who sold coffee publicly in England. His coffee-house was in George Yard, Lombard Street. In 1660, a duty was put on coffee. In the Christian, as in the Mohammedan world, the use of coffee met, at times, with vigorous opposition from the priests, who denounced it in many sermons still extant.

The first European author who speaks of coffee is Ranvolfo (in 1673). But Prosper Alpin was the first to describe the coffee-tree, in his "History of Egyptian Plants," published at Venice in 1691.

Let us now see at what period, and by what means, the coffee-tree was transported to Europe, and thence to America.

Boërhaave writes that Nicolas Witzen, a burgomaster of Amsterdam, and Governor of the East-India Company, having obtained, by means of the government at Batavia, some small plants grown from seeds from Mocha, planted them in the gardens at Amsterdam, where they grew and multiplied.

In 1714, the magistrates of that city sent a fine plant as a present to Louis XIV., and it was cultivated in the gardens at Marly. In 1718, the Dutch colony of Surinam began to plant coffee. In 1722, the French did the same in the Island of Cayenne; and, in 1727, at Martinique. In 1732, it began to be cultivated in Jamaica.

This was the foundation of the present trade in coffee with the West Indies.

OBSERVATIONS ON THE QUALITIES OF COFFEE.

It is generally admitted that the coffee of the Levant and of Asia is better than that of the West Indies. Its superiority consists in a finer aroma. Several admirable judges of coffee have observed the following facts: —

1st, That new coffee can never be so well roasted or prepared as that which is older. This arises from a certain viscous quality which the seed possesses when fresh.

2d, The smaller the grain, the better the coffee. It roasts better, and acquires more aroma.

3d, The larger and more succulent the seed, the worse the quality.

4th, The hotter and more arid the soil where it is grown, the more excellent is the coffee.

5th *(and this is well worthy of remark)*, The worst coffee grown in America will, in from ten to fourteen years, become equal to the best coffee of the Levant.

6th, Coffee grown in a dry soil, under a hot sun, and of the kind the seeds of which are small, will, in three years, be like that drunk in the best coffee-houses of London.

From this we may draw the conclusion, that excellent coffee might be grown in America if planted along the southern parts of the West-India islands; but, of course, the bulk of this superior coffee would be less, the seeds being so much smaller. But, besides this difference of form, there are other reasons for the greater excellence of Arabian coffee. In Arabia, the seeds are suffered to fall from the trees, when fully ripe, on cloths spread beneath them for the purpose. In the West Indies, they are gathered as soon as they begin to turn red. In the East, they dry the berries under cover, and without steeping; whilst, in the West, they macerate them in water for several days, and then dry them in the sun. Again: in Europe and America, cylinders are usually employed for roasting coffee in large quantities; whilst throughout Asia, the roasting being on a small scale, in private families, and done as often as the coffee is made (that is to say, at least twice every day), the process is performed in flat open pans, in which the seeds are kept shifted about until done ; whilst, in the household of the connoisseur, the roaster picks out each seed separately when it has acquired the proper degree of brownness. The last difference we will remark is, that, throughout the East (Turkey, Arabia, Persia, and India), the seeds are not *ground*, but pounded in a mortar until fine enough for use.

Oriental coffee, also, is never sent into the market so soon after it is gathered as that of the West Indies.

The Dutch inhabitants of Surinam are said to improve the flavor of their coffee by hanging it up.

Although we have spoken of the coffee-tree as requiring a dry soil, it must not be inferred that this is the case throughout the growth of the fruit. In fact, it is only when ripening that the berry requires this extreme dryness. During the earlier stages of its progress, the roots of the trees need to be kept constantly moist; and this is effected by small artificial streams, which can be turned off when the advanced state of the crop requires a dry soil. In some parts, even the full glare of the sun is injurious, and the coffee-trees are shaded by the spreading branches of a species of poplar planted at intervals among them for this purpose.

The discovery has been recently made that the leaves of the coffee-tree contain cafeine as well as the berries, and are used, dried like tea, by the natives of the East Indies. As the leaves are, of course, much more abundant than the fruit, should they really prove valuable, it will greatly reduce the price of coffee.

We will now proceed to the description of the different kinds of coffee obtainable in the markets. Of these,

MOCHA

takes the first place, from its superior aroma and flavor. The seeds are small, and of a yellow shade, and somewhat round. It is said that the withering of one of the two seeds in the fruit gives the other room to expand and take this form.

Mocha coffee is not so called because it is grown at Mocha, but because a French captain, in 1709, formed an establishment in that city for the purchase of the coffee of Ohdet, Betel-fagi, and other places, which was brought to Mocha for this purpose.

CAYENNE COFFEE

Is also in great favor. It resembles Mocha.

BOURBON COFFEE

Is large, long, pointed on one side, and of a whitish shade. It has less aroma than the two preceding kinds. It is brought from the Isle of France and Bourbon.

MARTINIQUE COFFEE

Is of medium size, greenish in color, of a bitter and herb-like taste.

ST. DOMINGO COFFEE.

Its green shade is paler than that of Martinique coffee: it is also dryer, and has less odor.

JAVA COFFEE

Is especially esteemed in the United States. It is less aromatic than the Mocha, and differs from it in flavor. The seeds are convex on one side, and flat on the other, full, and of a pale-green shade.

CEYLON COFFEE

Is also much esteemed by amateurs, though not so popular as the Java.

The coffee yield is by no means large. Manilla and Arabia produce about 4.500 tons *per annum;* Java, 60,000;

Ceylon and the British East Indies, 16,000; Cuba, 5,000; St. Domingo, 18,000; and Brazil, 142,000.

ON ROASTING COFFEE.

This operation is one of the most important for those who would obtain this beverage in a state of perfection: it will not be amiss, therefore, to say something on this subject.

When the seed is roasted in an enclosed vessel, it is a point of importance that it should never stand still, lest the coffee should be burned or scorched; in which case it loses its best soluble principles. Coffee, when roasted in large quantities, should be put into air-tight cylinders of iron; and the fire employed should be of dry wood, without any odor to it. It is for this reason that coal is not suitable for this purpose. The cylinder should be kept constantly turned, that every seed may be equally exposed to the heat. The roasting should be continued until the surface of the berries begin to shine, which indicates that the aromatic oil which does not exist ready formed in the plant, but is developed by the process, is completely matured.

In order to preserve the aroma of the coffee in the utmost perfection, a tea-dealer of London (Mr. Dakin, of St. Paul's Churchyard) has had his cylinders lined with silver, which he deems a great improvement on the ordinary iron-cylinders.

In all large establishments now, the cylinders are turned by steam-power.

The furnace most generally in use for roasting coffee is as follows: It is composed of a cylinder, and of a furnace in the form of an oblong box, both of strong plated iron. The cylinder has a latched door, which is opened to put in or take out the coffee, and to ascertain its progress. There is a square spit through the centre, extending beyond it at both its extremities, resting and turning on the edges of the furnace. At one end is a handle by which it is turned. The furnace is pierced by two holes at the back and front, which serve for the passage of air; and there are two handles at the ends, by which it may be lifted. In the interior is a grating, on which the wood or charcoal is placed. The furnace rests on four feet, which keep it a few inches above the ground.

But this machine is intended for roasting large quantities, and is not designed for private families, who, however, ought always to roast their own coffee, if they are particular about having it in perfection. As we have already mentioned, the Asiatics roast it fresh for every meal in flat open pans, over charcoal fires; and with us a perfectly clean frying-pan will answer all the purpose, the only care necessary to be taken being that the seeds should be kept constantly in motion until sufficiently roasted. Those that are first done should be removed from the pan, and allowed to cool while the others are being roasted. A small quantity of butter may be added while roasting.

The color of roasted coffee should be a chestnut-brown, very slightly blackened; and it should possess a peculiar and delicious odor. If more roasted than necessary to acquire this hue, it becomes carbonized, and loses its flavor. As a rule, it is better that it should be too little roasted than too much.

The roasting completed, and the coffee being cooled, you proceed to grind it; but this should always be done just when it is wanted, even if the roasting be performed in quantities, a practice unfavorable to the perfection of the beverage. An ordinary coffee-mill answers admirably, and may be bought for a small price.

The utensils for roasting and even grinding coffee are now frequently lined with porcelain, as are many other articles for the kitchen. No doubt the porcelain is exceedingly clean and nice while it remains perfect; and it is an advantage to the coffee-berry especially not to be brought into immediate contact with heated metal. But porcelain-lined articles are not only very expensive, but they never can be depended on. They are quite as liable to crack and fly in pieces the first time of using as the fiftieth; and, of course, are of no further service. We do not, therefore, recommend them; and we think it will be found, that, for all culinary purposes, cast-iron or copper vessels, kept perfectly clean, will give greater satisfaction.

Coffee, whether ground or unground, should be kept in closely covered tin vessels, to secure it from damp, which always destroys its flavor.

To secure good coffee, then, the following are essential: That the berry should be of a fine kind; have been properly packed; kept dry; be not too fresh; be well roasted, and somewhat finely ground. When ground large, the water does not so readily dissolve with the soluble principles.

COFFEE AS A BEVERAGE,— WHAT IT OUGHT, AND WHAT IT OUGHT NOT, TO BE.

Coffee, *properly prepared*, is one of the most refreshing of beverages. It seems to possess a peculiar charm to students, in clearing the brain and enlivening the faculties of the mind, inducing cheerfulness, and facilitating digestion. In various diseases, it has a peculiarly salutary effect, especially in asthma and nervous headache; and it is a powerful antidote to narcotic poisons. Coffee, also, is of great benefit to persons of sedentary habit, and those who are troubled with constipation.

But all these good qualities belong to *genuine coffee* prepared as an *infusion*, and are lost when the berry is adulterated with chiccory or any other foreign substance, and also when it is converted (*per*verted would be a more accurate word) into a decoction; that is, when it is *boiled:* and in this latter mode of preparation it is put on table in ninety-nine out of every hundred houses in England and America, and becomes the abominable drink which we know as coffee. No wonder it is so denounced by doctors as a slow poison, — very slow indeed, if properly prepared, it must be, since the most inveterate coffee-drinkers have lived to a great age.

Lay it down as a maxim, that no coffee can be good if it is boiled even for a minute. Water in a state of ebullition becomes more highly colored, indeed; but it fails to extract the delicate aroma and tonic properties of the powder; whilst the beverage into which it becomes converted is apt to produce flatulence, a sense of oppression, and many other physical discomforts, not to say positive injury.

The French, who, in modern times, are the great coffee-drinkers, and have made its proper preparation a profound study, are so sensible of the impropriety of boiling coffee, that they never attempt that process, but always either filter it with boiling water, or make use of one of the numerous *cafétières*, on the principle, more or less modified, of infusion by the pressure of steam; the water being, in these cases, boiled by a spirit-lamp forming part of the apparatus.

Many of these *cafétières* are imported to this country, and are more or less extensively used. But, generally, they have two faults, — that of being very complicated; and the further one of being liable to breakage when the part destroyed is not replaced without considerable difficulty and expense. This is especially the case with *cafétières* lined with porcelain, which is frequently cracked by the flames of the lamp beneath it; while to replace it is always expensive, and often impossible.

Some of the best coffee I ever tasted used to be made in the *cafétière plateau*, a coffee-pot introduced into England from France some twenty years ago. It consists of a very elegant bronze urn, with a glass vase above it fastened to the urn by a screw, while a ring of India-rubber makes it perfectly air-tight. From the vase, a tube extends nearly down to the bottom of the urn; and above it, in the bottom of the vase, is a fine perforated plate, on which the coffee is placed. A small screw admits air into the urn at pleasure, when the vase, which is screwed on, otherwise excludes it.

The quantity of hot water is to be measured into the vase, and the screw being slackened suffers it to fall into the urn. The screw is tightened again, and the coffee is then put into the vase (a small teacupful to somewhat less than a pint and a half of water), and the lamp lighted. As the water boils, it is forced up into the vase, where it bubbles among the coffee, looking exceedingly pretty, and diffusing the delicious and refreshing aroma through the room; and, when the lamp is extinguished, it descends into the urn, and is poured out by the faucet in the usual way.

It will be said that we have spoken against *boiled coffee*, and are now recommending the process we have forbidden; but the fact is, that this mingling of water, at boiling-point, with the powdered coffee, *at a distance from the heated bottom of the vessel*, has a totally different effect to that of ordinary boiling. The coffee is clear, hot, and full of aroma; in fact, just what it should be, which we may fairly call *perfection* in any beverage.

The strength of the coffee depends, of course, upon the taste of the consumer. It should be always served strong to strangers, as people in general are not supposed to like weak coffee. One cup of dry coffee to two cups of water makes the strongest coffee used: for ordinary family use, one small cup of ground coffee to a pint and a half of water is a good rule. At breakfast, cream or milk is generally used with coffee: these should be served, nearly boiling, in a covered pitcher, with the best double-refined sugar. Coffee-crushed, or common sugar, which is often served, destroys the fineness of the aroma, and materially injures the coffee. The coffee should be sent clear to each person at the table, and the cream and sugar served separately, that every one may mix the proportions to his taste. When cream or milk cannot be had, a lump of unsalted butter stirred into the coffee makes a tolerable substitute. A still better one is the yolk of an egg, beaten very smoothly with powdered sugar in the cup, then stirred with the coffee, which is poured slowly upon it. This, indeed, is preferred to cream by many amateurs in coffee, who also say that coffee should be made in advance, and heated over again before drinking, in whatever manner it may have been prepared. This operation demands care and attention, as the neglect of the smallest particular will spoil the coffee, which must be kept near the fire in a tightly closed coffee-pot, but must not be allowed to boil, or even to simmer, until the moment of drinking. It is necessary, besides, that the coffee-pot should be quite full, as, otherwise, it acquires a strong, rancid taste which is exceedingly disagreeable. The best coffee, reheated without care, loses its aroma and flavor.

BLACK COFFEE,

That is, coffee without cream or milk, should be taken after dinner — half an hour after is the best time — with sweet rusk or fine biscuit. Cream or milk destroys the beneficent digestive effects of coffee, on account of the relaxation of the stomach which they cause; and, therefore, should never be taken after a full meal. The white of an egg, stirred into the ground coffee with a little water before infusion, as well as clarified isinglass, is often used to clarify coffee; but this is not necessary when coffee is properly made.

COFFEE ROYAL

Is prepared in the following manner: Put four large lumps of loaf-sugar, or sugar-candy, into half a cup of strong coffee; then fill the cup with old cognac poured slowly over the back of a teaspoon. The spirituous liquor will naturally rise to the top: set fire to it in order to prevent its mixture with the coffee; and, when it has burned off, stir the liquid well, and drink it immediately. This liquor is drunk extensively in France, where it is commonly known as *gloria*, and is excellent for the digestion, though very stimulating in its effects.

Coffee, ½ cup; sugar, 4 lumps; cognac, ½ glass. Burn off the spirit.

COFFEE SHERBET

Is a delicious summer beverage, and is easily prepared. Make an infusion of one pound of freshly burned coffee in three quarts of soft water in the ordinary way, and, as soon as it is ready, pour it into an earthen vessel in which is two pounds of double-refined powdered sugar; cover it tightly; put it into a water-bath, and stir it from time to time. As soon as the sugar is thoroughly dissolved, pour it out, and leave it to cool; then freeze it; add five glasses of cognac brandy; stir the mixture thoroughly, and serve it for use.

Coffee, 1 lb.; soft water, 3 qts.; double-refined powdered sugar, 2 lbs.; cognac, 5 glasses.

FERAN'S SYRUP OF COFFEE.

Infuse four ounces of coffee in twenty-four ounces of pure cold water, in a tightly closed vessel, for six hours; then put it into a water-bath. As soon as the water boils, take out the vessel; let it stand for a while; then pour off the liquor, and add eight ounces of cold water to the dregs; pour this off, and add it to the first at the end of a few hours. Dissolve three pounds of double-refined sugar in a water-bath; strain it through a cloth, and stir it into the coffee, which is then fit for use.

Coffee, 4 oz.; pure water, 32 oz.; double-refined sugar, 3 lbs.

COFFEE LIQUEUR

Is a pleasant and wholesome beverage, particularly adapted to dyspeptics, as it facilitates digestion. It is prepared in tity than those of Soconusco, Caraccas, and Madeleine, which are generally sweet, and are worth, usually, about four times as much as the former.

The bark, or shell, of the cacao-nut contains, besides a large quantity of mucilage, a bitter principle, which transmits its flavor to milk when boiled in it, and forms, thus prepared, a favorite breakfast in Switzerland and Belgium. The shells are often ground and mixed with the nut to adulterate it.

WHAT CHOCOLATE SHOULD BE.

It frequently happens that chocolate is adulterated, not only with the ground shells, but with farina, starch, potatoes, lentils, roasted beans, ground almonds, sulphate of lime, chalk, and other pernicious substances; then highly perfumed with benzoin, Peruvian balsam, &c., to disguise the foreign taste. The residuum of the cacao-paste from which the vegetable butter has been extracted is often bought up at a low price, and made into chocolate with the addition of yolks of eggs, common butter, olive and almond oil, cocoa-nut oil, and even lard, mutton-suet, and tallow. Chocolate is also manufactured from beans that have been spoiled and rendered unwholesome by sea-water; and is not unfrequently colored with red and yellow ochres, red lead, vermilion, &c., when they become positively poisonous.

Many persons think that good chocolate thickens when prepared. This is a mistake; for this thickening only indicates the presence of farina. If, in breaking chocolate, it is gravelly; if it melt in the mouth without leaving a cool, refreshing taste; if it becomes thick and pasty on the addition of hot water, and forms a gelatinous mass on cooling,—it is adulterated with starch and similar substances. This may also be detected by dissolving the chocolate in boiling water, and, when cold, adding a few drops of aqueous solution of iodine: if farina is present, the mixture will turn blue; if pure, a yellowish-brown coloration will occur.

When earthy or other solid substances are deposited from chocolate mixed with water, either the beans have not been well cleansed, inferior sugar has been employed, or mineral substances have been added either to color it or to increase its weight. The analysis of this sediment will prove the nature of the mixture. Red or yellow ochre can be detected by the color; red lead can be detected by dissolving a portion of the sediment in nitric acid, and adding a few drops of solution of iodide of potassium, when, if lead be present, a yellow precipitate will form; and vermilion, by dissolving the sediment in nitric and hydrochloric acids, then adding dilute solution of the iodide of potassium, when the vermilion is detected by the formation of a scarlet precipitate.

If the chocolate has a cheesy taste, the vegetable butter has been extracted, and animal fat added. This chocolate soon grows rancid to the taste and smell.

If the chocolate be very bitter, sour, or musty, either the bean has been over-roasted or has been impregnated with sea-water. In either case, it is unfit for use.

In short, good chocolate should break without crumbling; should deposit a scanty, dull, fawn-colored sediment; should be of a clear dark-brown color, with a smooth, shining surface that does not tarnish on being touched; should have a fresh taste, dissolving readily in the mouth, and leaving a smooth mellow taste; and should be of medium consistency when diluted with water. Chocolate should be fresh, — at most, three or four months old; though very fine chocolates will sometimes keep for two years, and stand the test of sea-voyages tolerably well. Vanilla is the best flavoring substance, as it aids digestion, and heightens the tonic properties of the nut. Storax is sometimes used as a substitute: its presence is easily detected by the glutinous character which it gives the chocolate.

PREPARATION OF CHOCOLATE.

The primitive mode of preparing chocolate, as adopted by the Mexicans, was to roast the cacao-nuts in iron pots, crush them slightly, and remove the shells by fanning, bruise them to a paste between two heated stones, and then mix them with sugar and aromatics. From this simple process have sprung up many improvements in machinery, all based on these simple principles of slightly torrefying the nut, crushing it, and removing the shell, grinding it to a smooth paste, and incorporating it with various ingredients; then making it up into cakes, pastilles, &c. Various machines, moved by steam-power, are used in large establishments: but private families who wish to be sure of pure chocolate can easily manufacture it by simple apparatus; and, though they may not obtain chocolate of quite as beautiful an appearance, it will be equally palatable, and be free from all unwholesome ingredients.

Steep the nuts in water for four or five days, taking care to change the water twice a day, to remove any acidity or mustiness; dry them on sieves in the oven or stove till the shells are loosened; remove the shells, and expose the nuts in a coffee-roaster to a slow fire, turning them continually that they may roast evenly without burning. When thoroughly heated, take them out, winnow them to remove any shells that may be remaining, put them again into the coffee-roaster, increase the fire, and continue to turn them till they are of a shining-brown; take them out, winnow them again, then pound them in a mortar which has been heated with glowing coals to a smooth, oily paste; incorporate the requisite quantity of sugar (pound for pound for sweet chocolate), add whatever flavoring substance you prefer, and pound the whole together till the paste is perfectly smooth and liquid; then weigh it, and drop it into narrow tin moulds of the requisite size, which are placed in a tray in the oven or stove, and kept constantly in motion till the mass settles evenly in them, becoming smooth and shining, and filling the whole extent of the mould. Bubbles will often rise on the surface of chocolate prepared in this manner, owing to the air which has found its way in it in grinding. These may be expelled by pressing the paste firmly with the hand before putting it in the moulds. Machines arranged especially for this purpose are in use in the manufactories. Set the chocolate in the moulds to cool, remove them, wrap them in white paper, and keep them in a dry place.

The West-India cacao, the shells of which are detached with more difficulty, may be first heated in a coffee-roaster till the shells are loosened, then cracked in a mortar, and winnowed: they are then steeped in water for twenty-four hours to remove the acidity, the water being changed twice; then dried in the stove for twenty-four hours, after which they are reduced to paste as before described.

Having thus described the manner of preparing chocolate, it only remains for us to give the formulas in common use among confectioners, which are known by numbers; those numbered highest being of the finest quality. The farina used in the coarser kinds is employed to give greater consistency to the cacaos used in them; which is usually too liquid to run well in the moulds, and is incorporated with the addition of a few spoonfuls of simple syrup. Chocolate prepared in this manner, though inferior in quality, is not pernicious in its effects, like those vile compounds from which the fine oil of the nut has been extracted, and gross, fatty substances substituted in its stead. The formulas which we give here will be found important to all.

COMMON CHOCOLATE. I.

West-India cacao, 8 lbs.; dry brown sugar, 12 lbs.; farina, 5 lbs.

CHOCOLATE DE SANTÉ. II.

West-India cacao, 7 lbs.; very dry brown sugar, 10 lbs.; farina, 3 lbs.

CHOCOLATE DE SANTÉ. III.

West-India cacao, 7 lbs.; very dry brown sugar, 11 lbs.; farina, 2 lbs.

CHOCOLATE DE SANTÉ. IV.

West-India cacao, 7 lbs.; Martinique sugar, No. 2, 11 lbs.; farina, 24 oz.

CHOCOLATE DE SANTÉ. IV. HALF VANILLA.

West-India cacao, 7 lbs.; refined sugar, 10 lbs.; vanilla, 24 grs.; farina, 24 oz.

Pulverize the vanilla with a little sugar, and add it to the cacao in grinding: a little storax calamite may be added to increase the flavor of the vanilla.

CHOCOLATE DE SANTÉ. V. VANILLA.

Caraccas cacao, 3 lbs.; West-India cacao, 4 lbs.; refined sugar, 9 lbs.; vanilla, 4 drachms; farina, 1 lb.

CHOCOLATE. VI.

Caraccas cacao, 5 lbs.; Maragnon cacao, 2 lbs.; refined sugar, 7 lbs.; vanilla, 4 drachms; storax calamite, 3 drachms.

CHOCOLATE. VII. DOUBLE VANILLA.

Caraccas cacao, 7 lbs.; refined sugar, 5 lbs.; vanilla, 1 oz.

CHOCOLATE. VIII. FOR CHOCOLATE DROPS.

Maragnon cacao, 7 lbs.; refined sugar, 8 lbs.; farina, 1 lb.

CHOCOLATE. IX. FOR PASTILLES.

Caraccas cacao, 3 lbs.; West-India cacao, 4 lbs.; refined sugar, 7 lbs.; vanilla, 8 drachms.

CHOCOLATE WITHOUT SUGAR.

Caraccas cacao, 5 lbs.; Ceylon cinnamon, 5 drachms.

Grind the cinnamon fine, and add it to the cacao when reducing it to paste.

LADIES' CHOCOLATE

Is made of chocolate No. 6, manufactured in small moulds one inch long and two-thirds of an inch wide, then enveloped in fine paper, and ornamented with devices.

MARBLE CHOCOLATE.

Very pretty boxes, vases, &c., are made of chocolate manufactured in imitation of marble. This is done as follows: Expose No. 6 chocolate to a moderate heat; and, as soon as it begins to liquefy, rub it up with fine butter of cacao, thoroughly dissolved. Press the mixture firmly in moulds of the desired articles, and leave it to cool: the size of the veins in the marble depends on the quantity of butter used.

BAYONNE OR SPANISH CHOCOLATE

Is made by pressing out the butter of cacao, by rolling the cacao-nuts with a stone cylinder upon a stone slab heated by a furnace beneath it, mixing this butter well with sugar rolled upon the same slab, rolling the paste for the third time after adding the flavoring substances, then pouring it into moulds: this can be made without sugar. The Milan or Italian chocolate is prepared in the same manner.

TONIC SALEP CHOCOLATE.

Caraccas cacao, 5 lbs.; Maragnon cacao, 2 lbs.; refined sugar, 8 lbs.; powdered salep, 14 oz.

TONIC TAPIOCA CHOCOLATE

Is made after the same formula as the preceding, only substituting for the salep an equal quantity of tapioca.

TONIC SAGO CHOCOLATE

Is made in the same manner, substituting sago for salep, and using one pound less of sugar.

ARROWROOT CHOCOLATE.

West-India cacao, 6 lbs.; Caraccas cacao, 3 lbs.; powdered sugar, 10 lbs.; arrowroot, 11¼ oz.

This chocolate is excellent for consumptives; as also is Iceland-moss chocolate, prepared in the same manner.

WHITE CHOCOLATE.

Powdered sugar, 7 lbs. 10 oz.; tapioca, 1 lb. 12 oz.; oatmeal, 1 lb. 8 oz.; powdered Iceland moss, 8 oz.; concentrated tincture of Caraccas cacao, 8 oz.; tincture of vanilla, 2 drachms; distilled water from cacao-shells, 12 oz.

Mix the tapioca, oatmeal, and Iceland moss carefully, and add the tinctures of cacao and vanilla by degrees: when the mixture is complete, add the distilled water to form a smooth paste. This composition is suited to delicate persons, and those weakened by a long illness.

ANOTHER FORMULA OF WHITE CHOCOLATE.

Powdered sugar, 7 lbs.; tapioca, 1 lb. 12 oz.; oatmeal, 1 lb. 11 oz.; powdered Iceland moss, 1 lb. 4 oz.; concentrated tincture of Caraccas cacao, 8 oz.; tincture of vanilla, 2 drachms; distilled water from cacao-shells, 1 lb. 12 oz.

FERRUGINOUS CHOCOLATE.

Hydriodate of iron, 125 grains; chocolate paste, warm, 1 lb. This is an excellent tonic.

Having thus given the formulas of the various chocolates, we will proceed to the

MANNER OF PREPARING THE BEVERAGE.

There are as many different methods of drinking chocolate as of compounding it. The Mexicans are in the habit of drinking it with *atole*, a kind of pap, made of maize, which is their most ancient and common beverage, and which they mix hot, in equal quantities with the chocolate, dissolved in hot water, and drink directly.

They also dissolve the chocolate in cold water, stirring it with the chocolate stick, and skim off the froth into another vessel, then put the remaining chocolate over the fire with sugar enough to sweeten it, and, as soon as it boils, pour it over the froth, and drink it.

The inhabitants of St. Domingo put chocolate into a vessel with a little water, and boil it till it is dissolved, then add the necessary water and sugar, let it boil again till an unctuous froth is formed, and drink it in this state.

The Indians of New Spain make use of cold chocolate in their festivals, prepared by milling pure chocolate in cold water, skimming off the froth into another vessel, then adding sugar to the remaining liquid, and pouring it from a great height on the froth: this chocolate is exceedingly cold.

Iced chocolate is used in many parts of Italy, where it is the custom to cool almost all beverages upon snow or ice. This manner of drinking it is not disagreeable, as chocolate is unlike tea and coffee, which are only good when hot.

The Spanish method of making chocolate is to mix it so thick, that a spoon can stand upright in the mixture; then to drink iced water after it by way of diluting it.

Chocolate is usually milled in a tin vessel, within which a wheel, somewhat smaller in circumference than the vessel, is fixed to a stem which passes through the lid, and, being turned rapidly between the palms of the hands, bruises and mixes the chocolate with the water. Chocolate should be first milled off the fire, then put on and left to simmer for some time, after which it is milled again till perfectly smooth, and free from sediment. Any ladle or stick which effectually mixes the chocolate with the water may be substituted for the milling stick. Chocolate in powder does not require milling.

Chocolate should never be made until wanted, as it is spoiled by reheating.

Chocolate may be made in an iron pot or stew-pan, a chocolate-pot, or *chocolatière*.

WATER CHOCOLATE.

Put the necessary quantity of boiling water into the chocolate-urn, scrape or break a cake of chocolate for each cup into it, and take it from the fire. In ten minutes, the water will have penetrated the chocolate; uncover it, mill it until it is perfectly dissolved, then place it again on the fire, let it simmer for a minute, add sugar to the taste, and serve it with soda biscuit, rolls, toast, or cake. It is a mistake to suppose that chocolate needs to boil a long time : sugar and cacao being the bases of chocolate, the first gains nothing by boiling, and the second loses its perfume by evaporation. It is only when chocolate is incorporated with farina that it becomes necessary to boil it to cook the latter.

The Germans are in the habit of dissolving chocolate by steam, then letting it simmer for a moment, and serving it.

Chocolate, 1 cake; water, 1 cup; sugar to taste; boil up twice.

MILK CHOCOLATE

Is made by dissolving the necessary chocolate in the proportion of one cake to one-third a cup of water, then adding twice as much milk as water, and milling it with the chocolate-stick at the moment of pouring it out.

Chocolate, 1 cake; water, $\frac{1}{3}$ cup; milk, $\frac{2}{3}$ cup; boil up once.

GERMAN MILK CHOCOLATE.

Take one quart of milk, six ounces of chocolate dissolved by steam, and two ounces of powdered white sugar, and put them over the fire. Beat the yolks of five eggs to foam in a cup of cold milk, stir them into the chocolate as soon as it begins to simmer, let it simmer again, stirring it constantly, take it from the fire, and serve with sugar.

Chocolate, 6 oz.; milk, 1 qt.; yolks of 5 eggs; 1 cup cold milk; boil up twice.

CREAM CHOCOLATE.

Put a cup of boiling cream into a chocolate urn, with a cake of chocolate : as soon as the cream has softened the chocolate, dissolve it by the aid of the chocolate stick, let it simmer twice, and serve. Some persons dissolve the chocolate first in water, then add the cream and boil it to evaporate the water, losing at the same time the perfume of the chocolate.

Chocolate, 1 cake; boiling cream, 1 cup; boil up twice.

ALMOND MILK CHOCOLATE

Is made in the same manner as the preceding, slowly stirring a little orgeat syrup or paste into the chocolate after it is taken from the fire.

EGG CHOCOLATE.

Dissolve the chocolate in boiling water, beat the yolk of an egg to foam in a bowl, and pour the chocolate slowly over it, stirring it constantly all the time.

Chocolate, 1 cake; water, 1 cup; yolk of 1 egg.

GERMAN EGG CHOCOLATE.

Put four ounces of fine chocolate, dissolved by steam, into a perfectly clean stew-pan with three large cups of water, and one ounce of powdered sugar, and set it over the fire. Beat the yolks of two eggs to foam in a cup of water, and stir them, with fifteen drops of rose-water and the same quantity of orange-flower water, into the chocolate as soon as it begins to simmer : let it stand a few moments longer over the fire without boiling, stirring it all the time; then take it off and serve it with biscuit or marchpau.

Chocolate, 4 oz.; water, 3 cups; sugar, 1 oz.; yolks of 5 eggs; rose-water, 15 drops; orange-water, 15 drops; boil up once.

PARISIAN EGG CHOCOLATE.

For three cups of chocolate dissolve three ounces of the best chocolate in four cups of water, and set it over the fire; beat the yolks of two eggs to foam, and stir them into the chocolate as soon as it begins to froth; skim off the froth into warm chocolate-cups until they are heaped full, then hold a shovelful of burning coals to each till the froth is converted to a light crust; when serve.

The chocolate froths better when finely powdered sugar is mixed with the yolks of eggs, and still better when froth-cakes are added, prepared in the following manner:—

Beat the whites of a dozen eggs to froth, and stir in powdered sugar till the mass is of the consistency of a stiff paste. Mould the paste on a large plate into small cakes about the size and shape of an ordinary-size hazel-nut, and dry them in the sun or in a warm room.

As soon as the egg-yolks have been stirred into the chocolate, add as many of these cakes as there are cups of the liquid, and continue to stir it until the whole mass becomes froth. Care must be taken to keep the chocolate near the boiling-point, whether on or off the fire, without letting it boil over.

Chocolate, 3 oz.; water, 4 cups; yolks of eggs, 2; boil and mill to froth.

WINE CHOCOLATE.

Set half a bottle of good white wine, three ounces of chocolate, and one ounce of powdered sugar, over the fire; beat the yolks of four eggs to foam, with a little wine, and add it to the chocolate as soon as it begins to simmer; stir it for a few minutes, then take it from the fire and serve: this is an excellent winter beverage.

White wine, ½ bottle; chocolate, 3 oz.; sugar, 1 oz.; boil once.

HASTY CHOCOLATE.

A very good cup of chocolate may be prepared in haste by scraping a cake of chocolate into a cup, mixing it with the necessary proportion of sugar, then filling the cup with boiling water, and stirring the mixture; when it is ready to drink. The preparation of a cup of chocolate in this manner scarcely requires a minute.

CHAPTER XVIII.

TEA.

HISTORY OF THE PLANT.—ITS CULTIVATION.—PROPERTIES OF TEA.—ADULTERATIONS AND PREPARATIONS.—VARIETIES OF GREEN TEA.—HYSON.—OOLONG.—PEARL GUNPOWDER.—GUNPOWDER.—IMPERIAL SOUMLO.—BLACK TEAS.—BOHEA.—PEKOE.—CONGOU.—SOUCHONG.—FICHI.—TEA: WHAT TO DRINK, AND WHEN TO DRINK IT.—LADY-APPLE TEA.—TEA LIQUEUR.—ENGLISH TEA.—POLISH TEA.—ROSE-LEAF TEA.

HISTORY OF THE PLANT.

TEA is a shrub or tree of medium height, which flourishes from the equator to the forty-fifth parallel of latitude, and is cultivated chiefly in China and Japan. It derives its appellation from the native name, tscha, corrupted into té in the Tokien dialect. Linnæus classifies it into two species, *thea viridis* and *thea bohea*, which modern botanists have united into a single species, *thea chinensis*, attributing the varieties to the time of gathering, and method of drying the leaves. Tea was introduced into Europe from China by the Dutch, early in the seventeenth century. The infusion so rapidly grew into favor, that, in 1660, a tax of eight pence per gallon was imposed on it in England, which brought in considerable sums. The price of tea at this time was sixty shillings a pound. In 1641, Tulpius, a celebrated physician, the consul at Amsterdam, eulogized its good qualities, it is said, at the instigation of the Dutch East-India Company, who paid him a considerable sum for his laudations. In 1667, Jonquet, a French physician, repeated the eulogy; and, in 1668, Boutekoë, the physician of the Elector of Brandenburg, a man of high reputation, declared, in a dissertation which he published on coffee, tea, and chocolate, that it would not be injurious if drank to the extent of *two hundred cups a day*. This work was extensively read, and contributed not a little to extend the use of tea, which became very general before the end of the seventeenth century. Since that time, its consumption has increased to such an extent, that England now imports, for home consumption, about seventy million pounds; the United States, thirty-five million pounds; and France, twenty-five million pounds. In England and the United States, it is an indispensable beverage in all classes of society; while in France it is used very extensively, but chiefly for breakfast.

The tea plant is cultivated in plantations, and the leaves and buds are gathered in February, April, and June. The young and tender leaves of February are gathered with the greatest care, leaf by leaf, by persons especially detailed for this purpose, who are required to wear gloves, abstain from gross food, and bathe several times a day. These leaves, from the imperial or young hyson tea, possess the finest aroma of any; but this tea we know only from report, as it is wholly reserved for the imperial family, despite the imitations sold in market under its name. The second gathering takes place in April, and the third in June. In the last, the leaves are fully grown: the tea that they yield is of inferior quality, and forms the drink of the common people. The leaves are then dried on sheet-iron plates, moderately heated. The story that green tea derives its color from being dried on copper plates is without foundation, as none but iron plates are ever used. Green tea is made of younger leaves, of a finer quality: it is sometimes colored with Prussian blue and gypsum; but these adulterations are not in sufficient quantity to be poisonous. Black tea is the coarsest kind, with the largest leaves; and though it is considered more wholesome, because less stimulating, than green tea, we can conceive of no other reason than that it is less subtle.

Tea stimulates the action of the stomach, and facilitates digestion. Recent experiments by Böcker and Lehmann prove, that, with sufficient diet, the body is more likely to gain weight with tea than without it; and that, when the diet is insufficient, tea limits very much the loss of weight thereby entailed; as, by retarding the processes of dissimilation, it diminishes the rate of waste, and thus, though not directly nutritious, promotes the action of nutriment. This property, valuable in many circumstances, renders it evidently unfit for growing children, in whom the processes of assimilation and waste must be rapid, if healthful. But, on the contrary, a person of nervous temperament may be frequently invigorated and benefited by this subtle stimulus taken moderately in the morning, where the same amount at night would produce wakefulness and headache. In China, where the water is so bad that it is impossible to drink it except in an infusion of tea, the people are necessarily universal tea-drinkers; yet nervousness is not a characteristic of the celestials. In high-pressure America, we find it difficult to stop short of excess in one form or another. Temperance consists in using every stimulus moderately, a feat notoriously more difficult than total abstinence. In *temperance*, then, these three great beverages, coffee, chocolate, tea, may be used with advantage and pleasure.

Tea is often adulterated by being mixed with leaves of the ash and sloe. These mixtures may be easily recognized by an examination of the leaves after they have been steeped for twenty-four hours in water. The tea leaves will be found fringed with deep indentations, a soft, shining surface, and of a pale but bright green color; while the counterfeit leaves are rounder and more obtuse, the indentations are not so deep, the leaf is much less soft to the touch, the texture less delicate, and the color a deep olive-green. The leaves of different kinds of tea vary, it is true, in their size; but they all present the same form. Adulterated black tea, when moistened slightly, then rubbed on a sheet of white paper, leaves a bluish-black stain on it : it imparts a similar tint to cold water ; and this water reddens instantly on the addition of a drop or two of sulphuric acid. Put two ounces of tea in half a pint of soft water, and let it steep for two hours : the genuine tea will give an amber color, which will not be changed by sulphuric acid ; while the adulterated will make a black infusion, and redden, as we have described.

Green tea is sometimes colored with carbonate of copper, a highly poisonous substance. To detect this fraud, put a spoonful of the suspected tea into a vial with two spoonfuls of liquid ammonia and a spoonful of water ; cork the vial, and shake it well : the liquid will become a beautiful blue if there is the least particle of copper in the mixture. Green tea, colored with carbonate of copper, becomes black at once on being thrown into water charged with sulphuretted hydrogen, while the genuine tea experiences no change.

The quality of tea is injured by sea-voyages ; hence we may never hope to drink it in its perfection till we can receive it from China by the short route of Behring's Straits. The best tea drunk in Europe is that brought by caravans from China, by the way of St. Petersburg : this has a strong odor of violets, which tea brought over the sea never possesses. The tea imported into the United States has been brought hitherto almost exclusively from China ; but, since the recent commercial treaties with Japan, Japanese teas have been introduced into market, some of which are very choice, though their chief recommendation consists in their novelty.

The principal varieties of green tea are hyson, oolong, pearl gunpowder, gunpowder, imperial, and soumlo.

Hyson Tea.

Hyson, the coarser and finer qualities of which are known as hyson skin and young hyson, is green, with a tinge of bluish black. The leaves are curled lengthwise; the odor is peculiar and agreeable; the taste, sharp and astringent. When infused in water, the leaves unroll, and become of a brighter green; being oval in shape, smooth on one side, and downy on the other. The infusion is of a golden yellow color, with a pungent taste and aromatic odor: it reddens litmus paper, forms a white precipitate with the nitrate of lead, and black with the nitrate of silver; and has no action on the nitrate of barytes nor the oxalate of ammonia.

Oolong tea is said by Guibourt to be nothing more than hyson, aromatized by the flower of the *olea fragrans*, the *lauho* of the Chinese. It is one of the most esteemed varieties, and is much sought after by amateurs.

Pearl Gunpowder tea is closely curled, and almost round: its color is darker, and at the same time more grayish, than that of the oolong; and it has a more agreeable odor. Its leaves unroll more slowly in the boiling water, and are smaller than the preceding varieties. The infusion is more highly colored, and is a little turbid: the chemical properties are the same.

Gunpowder tea is still more closely curled than the preceding: the leaves from which it is prepared are cut transversely in three or four parts, then rolled up lengthwise very much like the hyson; being larger, however. The infusion has the same properties as that of the pearl tea.

Imperial, or Flowers of tea, has large, thin, glossy green leaves, of a faint but very pleasant odor.

Soumlo tea closely resembles the hyson: it has a leaden appearance and a very astringent taste, and takes its name from the place where it is cultivated.

The principal species of black tea are bohea, pekoe, congou, souchong, and fichi.

Bohea, the common black tea, of which there are two varieties, has leaves curled lengthwise, of a brown verging to black, with an odor less pleasant than that of the green tea. The leaves, when unrolled in boiling water, are lanceolate, dentated, and thicker than those of the hyson. Its infusion is less exciting than that of the latter; it is of an orange brown, with a bitter taste; it reddens litmus; precipitates without reducing the nitrates of silver and mercury; and turns the solutions of iron green.

Pekoe tea is a choicer variety of the bohea, having the same form and taste, with a more agreeable odor, resembling violets. The little silvery-looking threads which it presents are due to the undeveloped terminal leaves.

Congou tea has very large leaves, closely resembling the bohea in color and properties.

Souchong tea is a variety superior to the bohea, making a greenish infusion.

Fichi tea is dried crisp, then finely pulverized. It is prepared from the youngest leaves, and is never exported.

TEA. WHAT TO DRINK, AND WHEN TO DRINK IT.

There are as many different ways of drinking tea as coffee and chocolate. The Tartars moisten it with a glutinous substance, and mould it into cakes, from which they scrape off a portion for use, and boil it with butter, flour, milk, and salt. The inhabitants of Ava make of it a sort of pickle. The Chinese half fill a cup with tea, pour boiling water on it, and cover it with a saucer, let it stand for three or four minutes, then pour the infusion off, and drink it without milk, and usually without sugar. Sometimes they beat the yolk of an egg with sugar, then pour the tea upon it. They say that we injure tea by letting water stand too long upon it. The Russians drink it cold. In England, France, and the United States, it is always drunk hot, and usually with milk and sugar.

Tea may be made either in bright metal pots or urns, or in porcelain vessels. Bright metal is best, as, by its greater absorption of heat, it extracts at once all the properties of the tea. Tea made in porcelain pots must draw longer, and even then does not part with all its properties, as by pouring a fresh supply of water on the leaves after the first has been poured off, and letting it stand for some time, a second infusion may be obtained, nearly as strong as the first. This can never be done in bright metal tea urns, the leaves in which are worthless after the first infusion. Bright metal, therefore, is preferable, as making the tea better and more expeditiously.

Tea should never be boiled or suffered to stand long, as it thus acquires an unpleasantly bitter taste. The water should be boiling; if a single degree beneath the boiling-point, it will not extract the aroma and strength from the leaves.

To make tea, pour boiling water into the tea-urn, and let it stand for five minutes, that the metal may be thoroughly heated; throw it out, drain the urn, and put in it a teaspoonful of tea for each cup; pour on it from half to one cup of boiling water, according to the quantity of tea; let it draw for five minutes, then add water in proportion to the number of cups required.

Tea-urns differ but little from coffee-urns, being not quite so high, and larger in diameter. A small filter is inserted in the spout, which is opposite the handle, in order to prevent the tea-leaves from falling into the cups. The spout is closed by a cover, secured by a chain, to prevent the escape of the aroma; and the urn itself is closed at the top by a tightly fitting cover.

Put the cream, or milk, and sugar into the cups, and pour the tea on it, and serve. Cold unboiled milk or cream should be used, as hot milk destroys the aroma of the tea. Cream is far preferable to milk. Two teaspoonfuls of cream or double the quantity of milk should be used, though the quantity must be sometimes varied to suit exceptional tastes. If you use a porcelain teapot, have a covered pitcher of boiling water at hand, and fill up the pot after the tea is nearly drawn off.

Milk-tea may be made by substituting milk for water in the foregoing receipt. This is very nutritious, and will serve for a breakfast in itself.

LADY-APPLE TEA.

Pare, quarter, and core lady-apples; boil them for a few minutes in water, then take them out, let them drain, and throw them in sugar boiled to syrup; let them boil till they are cooked to conserves, then let them cool, and put them in jars, tightly closed. To obtain the infusion, make the quantity of tea required in the usual manner; put a dessert-spoonful of the prepared apples and syrup, for each cup, into a porcelain vessel; pour the boiling tea over it; let it cool a little, and serve. This is a refreshing beverage.

TEA LIQUEUR.

To obtain this agreeable drink, take four ounces of the best green tea, pour on it a gill and a half of boiling water, let it boil up a moment, then take the urn from the fire, and let it stand for a few moments to extract the properties of the tea. As soon as it is lukewarm, pour the infusion, which will be very strong, into a tightly closed jar containing two gallons of brandy, and let it steep for eight days. If, at the end of this time, the brandy has a strong odor of tea, with a violet perfume, it is well; if not, the tea used was not of good quality, and two ounces more must be infused in half a gill of water, then added to the brandy, and left for eight days longer. When this has been done, or when the brandy is sufficiently aromatized, boil it down one half in a water-bath; dissolve five pounds of refined sugar in four quarts of water, or, which is better, in four quarts of infusion of tea, add it to the brandy, and filter it. Tea liqueur prepared in this manner is a pleasant and mild beverage, and is excellent for digestion.

Tea, 4 oz.; brandy, 2 galls.; sugar, 5 lbs. Steep eight days, then boil down half.

ENGLISH TEA.

Make an infusion of one-fourth of an ounce of tea in a pint and a half of water; add a little vanilla and cinnamon; strain it through a cloth, and put it in an urn containing six or eight quarts; beat eight eggs and six yolks with three-quarters of a pound of powdered sugar; pour it on the tea, and stir it till it foams; then pour it into the cups, and serve. If you wish to add arrack, grate two lemons on three-quarters of a pound of sugar, and add it with liquor to suit your taste.

Tea, $\frac{1}{4}$ oz.; water, $1\frac{1}{2}$ pts.; vanilla; cinnamon; eggs, 8; yolks, 6.

POLISH TEA.

This is in reality a sort of beer, and is a very exhilarating winter beverage. To one quart of good white beer take one-fourth of a bottle of Rhine or any other white wine,— the Hungarian Pesti is good,— four or five ounces of sugar, the grated rind and half the pulp of a lemon, three or four yolks of eggs, half a glass of maraschino, and half a drachm of cinnamon. Set the beer over the fire, and, as soon as it boils up and froths, add the sugar and wine; next stir in the beaten yolks; then add the sugar, lemon, cinnamon, and maraschino.

White beer, 1 qt.; wine, $\frac{1}{4}$ bottle; sugar, 5 oz.; yolks of eggs, 4; maraschino, $\frac{1}{2}$ glass; cinnamon, $\frac{1}{2}$ dr. Boil up once.

ROSE-LEAF TEA.

A pleasant drink is made by substituting the dried petals of the centifolia, musk, or blush rose, carefully preserved as we have before directed, for tea, in an infusion either of milk or water. A little saffron, or a few drops of the tincture of cochineal, may be added to give the tea a rose-colored tint.

CHAPTER XIX.

LEMONADES AND ACIDULATED DRINKS.

Hot Lemonade. — Milk Lemonade. — Wine Lemonade. — 1 :ıtaric Lemonade. — Citric Lemonade. — Portable Lemonade in Cakes — Portable Lemonade in Powder. — Laville's and Fontenelle's Gaseous Lemonades. — Orangeade. — Acidulated Drinks. — Cherry Water. — Strawberry Water. — Raspberry Water. — Currant Water. — Raspberry Vinegar. — Strawberry Vinegar. — Currant Shrub.

LEMONADES.

In making lemonade, always choose the freshest and ripest lemons; rasp the rind with crushed sugar in order to extract the fine aromatic oil of the zest; then squeeze the juice, strain it, and add it, with the sugar, to the necessary quantity of water. Never use the rinds of the lemons, which only serve to impart a disagreeable bitter to the lemonade without adding to its strength.

For *Cold Lemonade*, rasp the rinds of three lemons with six ounces of sugar, dissolve it in a quart of cold water; add the strained juice of the rasped lemons with that of two Havana oranges.

Sugar, 6 oz.; lemons, 3; oranges, 2; water, 1 qt.

Hot Lemonade is made in the same manner, substituting boiling for cold water.

Milk Lemonade. — Rasp four lemons with six ounces of loaf-sugar, which dissolve in a pint of boiling water; add the juice of the lemons and a gill of sherry; stir the mixture well with three gills of cold milk, and strain through a jelly-bag.

Lemons, 4; sugar, 6 oz.; boiling water, 1 pt.; sherry, 1 gill; milk, 3 gills.

Wine Lemonade. — Rasp three lemons with a pound of loaf-sugar; put the sugar in a porcelain vessel, and pour on it boiling water enough to dissolve it; add two quarts of good red or white wine, and strain it through a cloth.

Lemons, 3; sugar, 1 lb.; water to dissolve; wine, 2 qts.

Tartaric Lemonade. — Take one drachm of powdered tartaric acid, four ounces of sugar, 1 drachm of the essence of lemon, and a pint and a half of water; mix the ingredients well, and filter for use.

Tartaric acid, 1 dr.; sugar, 4 oz.; essence of lemon, 1 dr.; water, 1½ pts.

Citric Lemonade. — Take 1 drachm of citric acid in powder, and four ounces of powdered sugar; dissolve in a pint and three gills of soft water, and flavor with one drachm of spirits of lemon. This powder may be kept and used as occasion requires.

Citric acid, 1 dr.; sugar, 6 oz.; water, 7 gills; spirits of lemon, 1 dr.

Portable Lemonade in Cakes. — Dissolve one drachm of gum arabic, and three drachms of tartaric, or, which is better, citric acid, in half a cup of water; add one pound of sifted sugar, and one drachm of essence of lemon; work the paste well together, put it in tin moulds rubbed with olive oil (each of which should contain an ounce), and set them in the stove. As soon as the cakes are dry, take them from the moulds, and keep them in a dry place. One cake makes two glasses of excellent lemonade. This preparation is very convenient for travellers.

Gum arabic, 1 dr.; tartaric acid, 3 drs.; sugar, 1 lb.; essence of lemon, 1 dr.; water, ½ cup.

Portable Lemonade in Powder. — Take one ounce of finely pulverized tartaric acid, add two pounds of finely sifted sugar, and two drachms of gum arabic finely powdered and flavored with a few drops of strong extract of lemon.

Laville's Gaseous Lemonade. — Two ounces of lemon-juice,

Acidulated Drinks.

four ounces of sugar, and twenty ounces of purest, strongest soda-water.

Lemon-juice, 2 oz.; sugar, 4 oz.; water charged with carbonic acid gas, 20 oz.

Fontenelle's Gaseous Lemonade.—Take one drachm of citric acid in powder, six ounces of powdered sugar, eight ounces of pure water, four drops of essence of lemon, and one and three-quarter pints of soda water; dissolve the sugar and the acid in the pure water, add the essence of lemon, divide the solution in bottles of twenty-ounces capacity, and fill them with the soda-water. This commercial soda-water contains five times its weight of carbonic acid gas.

Citric acid, 1 dr.; sugar, 6 oz.; pure water, 8 oz.; essence of lemon, 4 drops; water charged with gas, 1¾ pts.

When these gaseous lemonades are to be kept for a long time, a grain of the sulphate of soda should be introduced into each bottle. In this manner they can be preserved indefinitely. In a short time, the soda will be found to have entirely disappeared.

Orangeade.—Peel a ripe orange, cut it in thin slices lengthwise, and put it in a vessel with four ounces of sugar and a pint and a half of water; squeeze the juice of a lemon and two more oranges into another vessel; mix it well, and pour it on the orange, and let it stand a short time; then filter for use.

Orange sliced, 1; juice of lemon, 1; oranges, 2; sugar, 4 oz.; water, 1½ pts.

Lemonades can be prepared in the same way from currants, raspberries, strawberries, cherries, &c.

ACIDULATED DRINKS.

Pleasant and cooling drinks can be extemporized from fruits: these, however, must be used directly, as, not being fermented, they soon grow insipid.

Cherry Water.—Take the stones from two pounds of

sour red cherries, express the juice from the pulp into a porcelain vessel, add a little water and the juice of a lemon, stir it, and let it stand for two hours. Wash the stones carefully, pound them finely, and add to them the juice of the cherries, and eight ounces of sugar; strain the mixture, express the dregs to obtain any remaining liquor, stir the whole, and let it rest for twenty minutes, then filter, and put on ice.

Cherries, 2 lbs.; lemon, 1; sugar, 8 oz.

Strawberry Water. — Choose the largest and ripest berries; strip off the stems and hulls, and bruise them in a little water; let them stand in infusion for two hours, then strain through a cloth; put the juice into a bottle, and expose it, uncorked, for some time to the heat of the sun, or, still better, a stove. To half a pint of juice, add one quart of water and eight ounces of sugar; stir it well, and mix it by pouring it from one vessel to another, then set it on the ice.

Strawberry juice, ½ pt.; water, 1 qt.; sugar, 8 oz.

Raspberry Water. — Choose fully ripe raspberries; squeeze them in a cloth, let the juice rest, and pour it off clear; to half a pint of juice add one quart of water, and sweeten with from six to eight pounds of sugar; mix it well, strain, and put on the ice.

Juice of raspberries, ½ pt.; sugar, 8 oz.; water, 1 qt.

Currant Water. — Bruise a pound and a half of ripe currants in a mortar, taking care not to crush the seeds; add four ounces of bruised raspberries; put the whole in a glass dish, and expose it for some time to the sun or a hot fire; to half a pint of juice, take one quart of water and from six to eight ounces of sugar, and mix by pouring from one vessel to another; cool for use.

Currants, 1½ lbs.; raspberries, 4 oz.; sugar, 8 oz.; water, 1 qt.

Barberry Water is prepared in the same manner, only omitting the raspberries.

Acidulated Drinks.

Raspberry Vinegar. — Pour one pint of good vinegar on to a quart or three pints of ripe raspberries; let them stand twenty-four hours, then strain them through a jelly-bag, and add to the clear liquor another quart or three pints of raspberries, letting them also stand twenty-four hours more; strain again, and repeat the operation until the fruit has been added several times. When it has been finally strained, add one pound of white sugar to every pint of the liquor, and boil the whole in a porcelain-lined kettle for a half-hour. When cool, it may be bottled and kept in a cool place. It will keep for years; and a small quantity mixed with ice-water makes a most refreshing summer beverage, especially grateful to the sick.

Strawberry Vinegar. — Make like the above, only substituting strawberries for raspberries.

Currant Shrub. — To three pints of strained currant-juice add one pound of white sugar; boil fifteen minutes, scumming well; then take from the fire, and, when cool, add to every pint a teacupful of good brandy. Bottle, and cork tightly. This is used by mixing with ice-water according to taste.

CHAPTER XX.

LIQUEURS OR CORDIALS, AND SPIRITUOUS WATERS.

GENERAL REMARKS. — RATAFIAS. — ANISE-SEED RATAFIA. — ANGELICA RATAFIA. — BLACK-CURRANT RATAFIA. — ABSINTHE OR WORMWOOD RATAFIA.— ORANGE-FLOWER RATAFIA. — RASPBERRY RATAFIA.— RATAFIA OF RED FRUITS. — JUNIPER-BERRY RATAFIA. — POMEGRANATE RATAFIA. — GRENOBLE RATAFIA.— PINK RATAFIA.— NEUILLY RATAFIA. — SEED RATAFIA. — USQUEBAUGH. — SPIRITUOUS WATERS. — GENERAL DESCRIPTION. — COMPOUND ANISE-SEED WATER.— ANDAYE BRANDY.— AROMATIC WATER. — BERGAMOT WATER. — CINNAMON WATER. — CARAWAY WATER. — EAU DIVINE. — CLOVE WATER. — WATER OF PINKS. — MALTA WATER. — MINT WATER. — ALMOND WATER. — ROSEMARY WATER. — TEA WATER. — FINE ORANGE WATER.

LIQUEURS OR CORDIALS.

UNDER this name are comprised a great variety of preparations of alcohol, spirits of wine, and brandy, sweetened, and flavored with some aromatic substance. It is well known that simple liquors are produced by the fermentation and distillation of sugar, wheat, rye, rice, &c.; and by distilling the brandy, rum, or arrack, &c., produced from these, with one or more aromatic substances, then diluting it with water, and sweetening it with sugar or syrup, we obtain *compound liquors*, or *cordials*. *Ratafias* are produced by the simple infusion, instead of distillation, of the aromatics. Other varieties of liquors, under the names of *oils, creams*, &c., are also manufactured; but these only differ from the preceding in the quantity of sugar used, their composition being precisely the same.

To compound cordials which shall be soft, mellow, light, and transparent, none but the choicest materials, diluted with distilled, or at least filtered water, should be employed.

River water is always preferable to any other. The finest and whitest sugar should be used, especially for ratafias, which cannot be clarified during the operation; and to have cordials of every kind limpid, clear, and transparent, the sugar should be always boiled to syrup. The alcohol or spirits of wine should be rectified in advance, and be free from any empyreumatic odor. When brandy is used, it should be fourth-proof, and as old as possible; cognac, or, failing in that, Montpellier is the best.

To *filter* cordials clear, it is a matter of the first importance to have strainers felted with beaver, and fitted into a tin funnel with a closely fitting cover to prevent the escape of any of the aroma. Woollen strainers should never be used. When it is desired to make the cordial very transparent, the strainer must be coated with glue prepared as directed below. Some use brown or white paper for filtering; but this suffers the aroma to escape, and forms a paste which is apt to give a disagreeable taste to the cordial; besides, it needs to be often renewed, and thus causes a waste of time as well as of material.

To prepare the *glue* of which we spoke just now, take very dry, clear, and transparent isinglass, cut it as thin as possible, and dissolve it in white wine, stirring it with willow spirits until it is perfectly liquid; then put it into bottles, and preserve it for use. Coat the inside of the strainer lightly with it by means of a brush or sponge, then pour the liquor through the funnel. When one third has passed through, pour it back, and strain the whole again, as it is never so clear at the beginning as at the end of the process. Continue to pour it back until it becomes perfectly transparent; then strain it into bottles, and seal it tightly. This is the best method of obtaining cordial clear and limpid without losing any of its perfume by evaporation.

RATAFIAS.

These pleasant beverages are easily prepared either by the infusion in brandy of the expressed juices of fruits, or of the fruits themselves, nuts, and odorous flowers; to which are added various aromatic substances, and other ingredients susceptible of imparting a flavor to the liquor. Ratafias are much more easily prepared than cordials, as they require much less time, and do not exact the use of a distilling apparatus. As most fruits are very juicy, no other liquor than brandy should be used in fruit ratafias. To make the ratafia sufficiently aromatic, the berries should be bruised, the seeds pounded, and the flowers just withered, and steeped. When water is added, it is only to aid in dissolving the sugar. The length of the time of infusion should always be in proportion to the nature of the aroma: if too short, the flavor will be weak; if too long, the liquor will be bitter and acrid. To separate the ratafia, the liquor is decanted after infusion, and strained; but it should always be allowed to stand long enough to settle before bottling, or it will be thick and turbid, and will deposit sediment. All kinds of ratafia should be bottled, and closely sealed, and kept in a cool, shady place, both to prevent the evaporation of the spirits, and to hinder the slow but gradual decomposition of the liquor.

Anise-seed Ratafia. — Take two ounces of green anise-seed and four ounces of star anise-seed; bruise the seeds, and steep them in seven quarts of alcohol for eight days; then pass it through a sieve; add a syrup made with six and a half pounds of sugar and two quarts of spring water, and filter.

Green anise-seed, 2 oz.; star anise-seed, 4 oz.; alcohol, 7 qts.; sugar, 6½ lbs.; water, 2 qts. Steep eight days.

Angelica Ratafia. — Take four ounces of fresh angelica stalks, one ounce of angelica seed, one drachm of nutmeg,

Ratafias.

half a drachm of Ceylon cinnamon, and one drachm of coriander; bruise the seeds in a mortar, and steep the whole for eight days in seven pints of alcohol; then pass it through a sieve; add a syrup made with four and a quarter pounds of sugar and two and a half pints of water, and filter.

Angelica stalks, 4 oz.; angelica seed, 1 oz.; nutmeg, 1 dr.; cinnamon, $\frac{1}{2}$ dr.; coriander, 1 dr.; sugar, $4\frac{1}{2}$ lbs.; water, $2\frac{1}{2}$ pts. Steep eight days.

Black-Currant Ratafia. — Take six pounds of fully ripe black currants, four ounces of black-currant leaves, half a drachm of cloves, half a drachm of Ceylon cinnamon, and half a drachm of coriander; bruise the berries, and steep the whole for one month in ten quarts of brandy; then express the liquor; add a syrup made with seven pounds of sugar and three and a half pints of water, and filter.

Black currants, 6 lbs.; black-currant leaves, 4 oz.; cloves, $\frac{1}{2}$ dr.; cinnamon, $\frac{1}{2}$ dr.; coriander, $\frac{1}{2}$ dr.; sugar, 7 lbs.; water, $3\frac{1}{2}$ pts. Steep one month.

Absinthe or Wormwood Ratafia. — Steep four pounds of bruised wormwood leaves, eight ounces of juniper berries, and two ounces of ground cinnamon, in four drachms of angelica rum and seventeen pounds of brandy, for fifteen days; distil the mixture to twelve pounds of liquor, and redistil this upon the residuum to ten pounds; then· add two and a half pounds of powdered sugar, two pounds of pure water, and eight ounces of double-distilled orange-flower water.

Wormwood leaves, 4 lbs.; juniper berries, 8 oz.; cinnamon, 2 oz.; angelica rum, 4 drs.; brandy, 17 lbs.; sugar, $2\frac{1}{2}$ lbs.; water, 2 lbs.; orange-flower water, 8 oz. Steep fifteen days.

Orange-flower Ratafia. — Steep two pounds of bruised orange blossoms in ten and a half pints of alcohol for fifteen days; add a syrup made with four pounds of sugar and seven gills of water, and filter.

Orange flowers, 2 lbs.; alcohol 10½ pts.; sugar, 4 lbs.; water, 7 gills. Steep fifteen days.

Raspberry Ratafia. — Steep eight pounds of raspberries for fifteen days in two gallons of brandy; add a syrup made with seven pounds of sugar and three quarts of water, and filter.

Raspberries, 8 lbs.; brandy, 2 gals.; sugar, 7 lbs.; water, 3 qts. Steep fifteen days.

Ratafia of Red Fruits. — Infuse one pound of sour cherries, one pound of black cherries, one pound of wild cherries, one pound of raspberries, one pound of red currants, and three pounds of strawberries, in two and a half gallons of brandy for fifteen days; add a syrup made with eight pounds of sugar, and filter.

Sour cherries, 1 lb.; black cherries, 1 lb.; wild cherries, 1 lb.; raspberries, 1 lb.; red currants, 1 lb.; strawberries, 1 lb.; brandy, 2½ gals.; sugar, 8 lbs. Steep fifteen days.

Juniper-Berry Ratafia. — Take eight ounces of juniper berries, one drachm of cinnamon, two drachms of coriander, and half a drachm of mace; bruise the whole, and steep them for fifteen days in fourteen pints of brandy; squeeze through a cloth, and add a syrup made with seven pounds of sugar, and filter.

Juniper-berries, 8 oz.; cinnamon, 1 dr.; coriander, 2 drs.; mace, ½ dr.; brandy, 14 pts.; sugar, 7 lbs. Steep fifteen days.

Pomegranate Ratafia. — Steep fifteen fully ripe pomegranates, cut in slices, in four quarts of brandy, for fifteen days; squeeze through a cloth; add a syrup made with three pounds of sugar, and filter.

Pomegranates, 15; brandy, 4 qts.; sugar, 3 lbs. Steep fifteen days.

Grenoble Ratafia. — Take eight quarts of black wild-cherry juice, two drachms of cinnamon, one drachm of cloves, one drachm of mace, twelve ounces of cherry-leaves, and four pounds of black cherries; steep the whole in seven quarts of alcohol for twenty days; squeeze through a cloth; add nine pounds of crushed sugar, and filter as soon as it is dissolved.

Wild-cherry juice, 8 qts.; cinnamon, 2 drs.; cloves, 1 dr.; mace, 1 dr.; cherry leaves, 12 oz.; wild cherries, 4 lbs.; sugar, 9 lbs. Steep twenty days.

Walnut Ratafia. — Steep sixty freshly cracked walnuts with thirty-seven grains of clove and an equal quantity of mace and cinnamon in five quarts of alcohol for two months; express the juice, and add a syrup made with five pounds of sugar. This ratafia improves with age.

Walnuts, 60; clove, 37 gr.; mace, 37 gr.; cinnamon, 37 gr.; alcohol, 5 qts.; sugar, 5 lbs. Steep two months.

Pink Ratafia. — Take two pounds of the petals of red pinks, one drachm of cinnamon, and one drachm of cloves; steep the whole in seven pints of alcohol for fifteen days; strain; add a syrup made with two pounds of sugar, and filter.

Pinks, 2 lbs.; cinnamon, 1 dr.; cloves, 1 dr.; alcohol, 7 pts.; sugar, 2 lbs. Steep fifteen days.

Neuilly Ratafia. — Steep five pounds of sour cherries, two pounds of black cherries, and one pound of the petals of red pinks, in fourteen pints of brandy, for fifteen days; strain, and add one-fourth of a pound of sugar to every quart of liquor.

Sour cherries, 5 lbs.; black cherries, 2 lbs.; pink petals, 1 lb.; brandy, 14 pts.; sugar according to quantity. Steep fifteen days.

Seed Ratafia. — Take one ounce each of dill, angelica, fennel, caraway, carrot, coriander, and green anise seed; pound them, and steep them for a month in six quarts of alcohol; strain, and add a syrup of eight pounds of sugar with one quart of water; then filter.

Dill, angelica, fennel, caraway, carrot, coriander, and anise seeds, 1 oz. each ; alcohol, 6 qts.; sugar, 8 lbs.; water, 1 qt. Steep one month.

Usquebaugh. — Steep one ounce of saffron, half a drachm of mace, and the yellow rinds of four oranges and two lemons, in two gallons of alcohol, for one month ; strain ; add a syrup made with nine pounds of sugar and one quart of water, and filter.

Saffron, 1 oz.; mace, ½ dr.; zests of oranges, 4 ; zests of lemon, 2 ; alcohol, 2 gals.; sugar, 9 lbs.; water, 1 qt. Steep one month.

SPIRITUOUS WATERS.

The various preparations designated by the name of *waters*, which are used so largely at present, are generally obtained by the infusion of one or more substances in alcohol, the strength of which is proportioned to the nature of the ingredients infused and the object sought to be attained. It usually suffices to put the material that is to serve for the basis of the liquor into a vessel, and pour on it the alcohol, which must be of proof-strength, containing fifty per cent of pure alcohol, and perfectly colorless. It is then left in cold infusion, or at the temperature of the atmosphere, for a greater or less time. Occasionally, it is necessary to use heat, and to distil the liquor. But, whatever may be the process employed, the substances infused must always be divided, crushed, reduced to powder, or cut in small pieces; and the vessel must be stopped up with a cork, or a piece of kid pierced with small holes. Sometimes it is necessary to shake it from time to time to facilitate the solution ; and, when this is complete, the liquor must be carefully filtered. When the alcohol is to hold a number of substances in suspension, they must not be submitted together to its action, but successively, according to their degree of solubility; or else a portion of the spirits of wine must be reserved, then added when the first has been poured off and filtered.

The infusions made in alcohol differ greatly in taste, odor, color, and virtues. They are simple and compound, some containing aromatic, oily substances, which whiten or grow turbid on the addition of water; others containing nothing but extractive, sugared substances, and giving no precipitate when water is added. The infusion or immersion, for a greater or less time, in wine-water, vinegar, or alcohol, when made in cold, is called *maceration;* when made with heat, but below boiling-point, *digestion*. They differ, besides, essentially, through the nature of the liquor which gives them strength, being acetous, aqueous, spirituous, and vinous. Under the name of *spirituous waters*, we comprise all those which are made by the addition and mixture of brandy with different substances which combine with it, and give it a peculiar taste, odor, and virtues.

Compound Anise-seed Water. — Rub four ounces each of green anise, angelica, and star anise seed, to a very fine powder in a mortar; macerate the whole in five pints of alcohol for five or six days; then distil in a water-bath.

Green anise, angelica, and star anise seed, each, 4 oz.; alcohol, 5 pts. Macerate six days.

Andaye Brandy. — Macerate an ounce each of green and star anise seed, two ounces of coriander, and one ounce of powdered iris, with the yellow rinds of four oranges, in ten pints of Spanish brandy, for eight days; then distil* in a water-bath; add a syrup made with five pounds of sugar, and filter.

Green and star anise seed, each, 1 oz.; coriander, 2 oz.;

---

* For the benefit of those who are not familiar with the process of distillation, it may be remarked that it essentially consists in collecting the steam arising from any boiling liquid in a cold vessel that will condense it to liquid again. It serves to separate liquids from undistillable solids (that is, which cannot be converted into steam), and also to separate different liquids from each other, according to their relative boiling-points. A common chemical apparatus consists of a glass retort, in which the liquid is placed and boiled. The neck of the retort is inserted into any convenient vessel, usually of glass, that is, covered with ice; and the steam, passing into that, falls in drops into the receiver. The heat must not be applied immediately to the retort, but that placed in a vessel of water (a saucepan would do), and the heat placed under that. Thus is constituted, at moderate expense, a water-bath and still; but it may be varied at pleasure.

iris, 1 oz.; Spanish brandy, 10 pts.; sugar, 5 lbs.; zests of 4 oranges. Macerate eight days.

Aromatic Water. — Macerate one ounce of pounded cinnamon, three drachms of cardamom, four drachms of sassafras, and one drachm of ginger, for eight days, in five pints of alcohol; then distil in a water-bath.

Cinnamon, 1 oz.; cardamom, 3 drs.; sassafras, 4 drs.; ginger, 1 dr.; alcohol, 5 pts. Macerate eight days.

Bergamot Water. — Macerate the yellow rinds of four bergamots, four oranges, and two lemons, in ten pints of alcohol, for eight days; then distil to one-half the quantity in the water-bath, and add a syrup made with four pounds of fine sugar and three pints of water.

Zests of bergamot, 4; zests of orange, 4; zests of lemon, 2; alcohol, 10 pts.; sugar, 4 lbs.; water, 3 pts. Macerate eight days.

Cinnamon Water. — Macerate two ounces of pounded cinnamon, ten drops of essence of lemon, and the yellow rind of two oranges, in seven quarts of alcohol, for eight days; then distil in the water-bath, and add a syrup made with eight pounds of sugar and two quarts of water. Color yellow.

Cinnamon, 2 oz.; essence of lemon, 10 drops; zests of orange, 2; alcohol, 7 qts.; sugar, 8 lbs.; water, 2 qts. Steep eight days.

Caraway Water. — Macerate four ounces of pounded caraway-seeds in seven pints of alcohol for eight days; then distil in the water-bath, and add a syrup made with four pounds of sugar and three pints of water. Filter, and color green.

Caraway, 4 oz.; alcohol, 7 pts.; sugar, 4 lbs.; water, 3 pts. Macerate eight days.

Eau Divine. — Macerate the zests of three limes and four lemons with four ounces of fresh orange-flowers, one ounce of fresh heads of balm, and six ounces of white hoarhound, in seven pints of alcohol, for ten days; distil in the water-bath, and add a syrup made with three pounds of sugar and one quart of distilled water.

Zests of limes, 3; zests of lemons, 4; orange-flowers, 4 oz.; balm, 1 oz.; hoarhound, 6 oz.; alcohol, 7 pts.; sugar, 3 lbs.; distilled water, 1 qt. Steep ten days.

Clove Water. — Take one ounce of pounded cloves, one drachm of mace, seven pints of alcohol, and four pounds of sugar. Proceed as in the last, and color yellow.

Water of Pinks. — Macerate one pound of the petals of red pinks and half a drachm of pounded cloves in ten pints of alcohol for eight days; distil in the water-bath; add a syrup made with five pounds of sugar and three pints of water, and color a deep red.

Pinks, 1 lb.; cloves, ½ dr.; alcohol, 10 pts.; sugar, 5 lbs.; water, 3 pts. Steep eight days.

Malta Water. — Macerate the zests of six oranges with four ounces of fresh orange-flowers in seven pints of brandy for eight days; distil in the water-bath; add a syrup made with four pounds of sugar and three pints of water, and filter.

Zests of oranges, 6; orange-flowers, 4 oz.; brandy, 7 pts.; sugar, 4 lbs.; water, 3 pts. Steep eight days.

Mint Water. — Steep two pounds of peppermint-blossoms, with the yellow rinds of four lemons, in six quarts of alcohol, for eight days; distil in the water-bath; add a syrup made with nine pounds of sugar and three pints of water; to which is added half a pint of rose-water, and filter.

Peppermint-flowers, 2 lbs.; zests of lemons, 4; alcohol, 6 qts.; sugar, 9 lbs.; water, 3 pts.; rose-water, ½ pt. Steep eight days.

Almond Water. — Macerate four ounces of bitter almonds, with four ounces each of apricot, peach, and cherry stones, in seven pints of alcohol, for one month; distil as before; add a syrup made with three pounds of sugar, and filter.

Bitter almonds, 4 oz.; peach-stones, 4 oz.; apricot-stones, 4 oz.; cherry-stones, 4 oz.; brandy, 7 pts.; sugar, 3 lbs. Steep one month.

Rosemary Water. — Macerate eight ounces of rosemary blossoms in three pints of alcohol for ten days; then distil in the water-bath to perfect dryness.

Rosemary, 8 oz.; alcohol, 3 pts.

Tea Water. — Distil one ounce of hyson and half an ounce of souchong tea in seven pints of alcohol by means of the water-bath; add a syrup made with two pounds of sugar and a quart of distilled water, and filter. This can also be made by infusion.

Hyson, 1 oz.; souchong, ½ oz.; alcohol, 7 pts.; sugar, 2 lbs.; distilled water, 1 qt.

Fine Orange Water. — Macerate the yellow rinds of a dozen oranges in ten pints of highly rectified spirits for fifteen days; add one drachm of neroli; distil in the water-bath, and add a syrup made with four pounds of sugar and one quart of water, and filter.

Zests of orange, 12; neroli, 1 dr.; alcohol, 10 pts.; sugar, 4 lbs.; water, 1 qt. Steep fifteen days.

CHAPTER XXI.

SPIRITUOUS CREAMS, ELIXIRS, MISCELLANEOUS LIQUEURS, AND DOMESTIC WINES.

WHAT CREAMS ARE. — ABSINTHE CREAM. — BARBADOES CREAM. — COCOA CREAM. — FRUIT CREAM. — ORANGE-FLOWER CREAM WITH MILK AND CHAMPAGNE. — JASMINE CREAM. — CHERRY-WATER CREAM. — LAUREL CREAM. — MINT CREAM. — MYRTLE CREAM. — MOCHA CREAM. — CREAM OF ROSES. — VANILLA CREAM. — CHOCOLATE CREAM. — ELIXIRS. — JUNIPER-BERRY ELIXIR. — ELIXIR OF GARUS. — TROUBADOUR'S ELIXIR. — TABOUREY ELIXIR. — ELIXIR OF VIOLETS. — MISCELLANEOUS LIQUEURS. — ANISETTES. — ANISETTES DE BOURDEAUX. — BALM OF MANKIND. — CITRONELLE. — CURAÇOA. — OLD MEN'S MILK. — NECTAR. — USQUEBAUGH. — PERFECT LOVE. — PERSICOT. — DOMESTIC WINES. — CURRANT WINE. — BLACKBERRY WINE. — GOOSEBERRY WINE. — ELDERBERRY WINE. — STRAWBERRY WINE. — RASPBERRY WINE. — RHUBARB WINE.

CREAMS.

ALL spirituous liquors, whether charged or not with bitter extractive substances, when mixed with white sugar in the form of syrup, and heated to the boiling-point, become fat and unctuous; from which essential qualities they take the name of *creams.* They are as numerous as varied, and are much sought after, both on account of their agreeable taste, and because their stimulus is less powerful and exhausting than that of spirits pure, or mixed simply with water.

Absinthe or Wormwood Cream. — In seven pints of common brandy infuse, for two days, half a pound of the heads of wormwood and the zests of two lemons, or, which is better, two oranges thinly sliced; distil the liquor to half the quantity; dissolve six pounds of fine sugar in three pints of common water; let it cool, and mix it well with the brandy; strain it, and put in bottles tightly corked.

Wormwood, ½ lb.; oranges, 2 ; brandy, 7 pts.; sugar, 6 lbs.; water, 3 pts.   Infuse two days.

Barbadoes Cream. — Infuse for five or six days, in two quarts of brandy, two drachms each of mace and cinnamon and the zests of two limes ; distil the liquor to one-half over a gentle fire ; dissolve three pounds of sugar in a quart of water over the fire, let it cool, mix the whole together, add half a pound of orange-flower water, strain it, and keep it in tightly corked bottles.

Mace, 2 drs.; cinnamon, 2 drs.; zests of limes, 2 ; brandy, 2 qts.; sugar, 3 lbs.; water, 1 qt.; orange-flower water, ½ lb. Infuse six days.

Cocoa Cream. — Pound two pounds of roasted cacao-nuts in a stone mortar ; mix with them two quarts of brandy; add two drachms of cinnamon, and let it steep for eight days ; then distil the liquor to one-half. Dissolve two and a half pounds of sugar in a quart of water over the fire ; mix the whole, let it cool, then add one and a half drachms of tincture of vanilla ; filter, and bottle for use.

Cacao-nuts, 2 lbs. ; cinnamon, 2 drs.; brandy, 2 qts. ; sugar, 2½ lbs.; water, 1 qt.; vanilla, 1½ drs.

Fruit Cream. — Cut very thin the rind and zests of two bergamots, two Seville oranges, two limes, two lemons, and three oranges ; macerate the whole for eight days in seven pints of fourth-proof brandy ; then distil the liquor to nearly one-half. Dissolve four pounds of sugar in three pints of water; let it cool ; mix the whole thoroughly; filter, and bottle for use.

Bergamot, 2; oranges, 2; limes, 2; lemons, 2; oranges, 3; brandy, 7 pts.; sugar, 4 lbs.; water, 3 pts.   Steep eight days.

Orange-Flower Cream with Milk and Champagne Wine. — Put three pints of new milk over the fire ; add fourteen ounces of orange-blossoms ; let it boil up once or twice, then pour it into a porcelain vessel to cool. As soon as it is quite cold, add a quart of rectified brandy; stir the mixture, and filter it to separate the orange-flowers, which are now deprived of their aroma, and contain nothing but bitterness. Dissolve four pounds of double-refined sugar in three pints of water over the fire; let it cool, and mix with it seven pints of good champagne; add the milk, and filter again.

This process is far preferable to making a simple infusion of the orange-flowers in the liquor, which is always bitter and acrid; or to distilling it in order to obtain what is called the *spirit*, in which case it loses the greater part of its taste and aroma.

Milk, 3 pts.; orange-flowers, 14 oz.; brandy, 1 qt.; sugar, 4 lbs.; water, 3 pts.; champagne, 7 pts.

Jasmine Cream. — Dissolve over the fire two pounds of double-refined sugar in a quart of water; let it cool, and add three ounces of double-distilled tincture of jasmine, four drachms of orange-flower water, and one and a half pints of alcohol; mix the whole well, filter, and bottle for use.

Sugar, 2 lbs.; water, 1 qt.; jasmine, 3 oz.; orange-flower water, 4 drs.; alcohol, $1\frac{1}{2}$ pts.

Cherry-water Cream. — Distil seven pints of cherry-water to nearly one-half; add four ounces of orange-flower water. Dissolve over the fire four pounds of sugar in a quart of spring-water; let it cool; add it to the cherry-water, and strain the whole. This is a delicious beverage, which may be kept in tightly corked bottles for a long time without the slightest deterioration.

Cherry-water, 7 pts.; orange-flower water, 4 oz.; sugar, 4 lbs.; water, 1 qt.

Laurel Cream. — Distil seven ounces of laurel-leaves, five ounces of myrtle-blossoms, half a nutmeg coarsely grated, and twenty-four cloves which have been first infused for ten hours in two gallons of brandy; distil to half the liquor. Dissolve over a gentle fire twelve pounds of sugar in seven pints of water; let it cool; mix the whole well, filter it. and preserve it in tightly corked bottles.

Laurel-leaves, 7 oz.; myrtle-flowers, 5 oz.; cloves, 24; brandy, 2 gals.; nutmeg, ½; sugar, 12 lbs.; water, 7 pts.

Mint Cream. — Take one pound of freshly gathered mint, and the zests of five lemons; cut fine; macerate them for eight days in seven pints of brandy; distil to one-half, then add half a drachm of essence of peppermint. Dissolve four pounds of sugar in three pints of water, let it cool; mix it thoroughly with the distilled liquor, filter, and keep it in bottles in a cool and shady place.

Mint, 1 lb.; zests of lemons, 5; brandy, 7 pts.; essence peppermint, 2 drs.; sugar, 4 lbs.; water, 3 pts. Steep eight days.

Myrtle Cream. — Macerate six ounces of myrtle-blossoms or leaves, one ounce of peach-leaves, and one-quarter of a nutmeg coarsely grated, in seven pints of brandy, for two days; distil to one-half; mix it thoroughly with four pounds of sugar dissolved over the fire in three pints of water; filter, and bottle for use. This cream, which is very bitter at first, becomes a delightful beverage with age.

Myrtle-leaves, 6 oz.; peach-leaves, 1 oz.; nutmeg, ¼; brandy, 7 pts.; sugar, 4 lbs.; water, 3 pts. Infuse two days.

Mocha Cream. — Roast one pound of good Mocha coffee slightly without letting it brown, grind it quickly without giving it time to grow cold, and infuse it, with the yellow rind of an orange cut fine, in seven pints of brandy, for five or six days; then distil it nearly to one-half in the water-bath. Dissolve four pounds of sugar over the fire in three pints of water, let it cool, mix it with the coffee mixture, filter, and preserve in well-corked bottles.

Mocha coffee, 1 lb.; zest of orange, 1; brandy, 7 pts.; sugar, 4 lbs.; water, 3 pts. Infuse six days.

Cream of Roses. — Macerate three pounds of rose-leaves in two quarts of good brandy for five or six days; distil the

Elixirs.

liquor to one-half in the water-bath; mix it thoroughly with one pound of sugar dissolved in a quart of water, or, which is better, in rose-water enough to dissolve it; color with a little cochineal, and filter.

Rose-leaves, 3 lbs.; brandy, 2 qts.; sugar, 1 lb.; water, 1 qt. Infuse six days.

Vanilla Cream. — Infuse four drachms of tincture of vanilla and half a drachm of tincture of amber in seven pints of alcohol; dissolve five pounds of sugar over the fire in a quart of pure water; let it cool; mix the whole, and filter. This may be colored red or violet.

Tincture of vanilla, 4 drs.; tincture of amber, ½ dr.; alcohol, 7 pts.; sugar, 4 lbs.; water, 1 gal.

Chocolate Cream. — Take six pounds of pure Caraccas chocolate, six drachms of ground cinnamon, and two gallons of alcohol; distil to one-half; add ten pounds of sugar dissolved in four quarts of distilled water, and four drachms of tincture of vanilla, and filter.

Chocolate, 6 lbs.; cinnamon, 6 drs.; alcohol, 2 gals.; sugar, 10 lbs.; distilled water, 4 qts.; tincture of vanilla, 4 drs.

ELIXIRS.

Juniper-Berry Elixir. — Macerate two ounces of juniper-berries in two quarts of alcohol for one month; strain the liquor, and add a syrup made with three pounds of sugar and a pound and a half of water.

Elixir of Garus. — Myrrh and aloes, each, two drachms; cloves and nutmeg, each, 3 drachms; saffron, one ounce; cinnamon, five drachms. Macerate the whole for fifteen days in four quarts of alcohol; distil in the water-bath, and add a syrup made with six pounds of sugar. This liquor can also be made without distillation.

Troubadours' Elixir. — Musk roses, two pounds; jasmine blossoms, twelve ounces; orange-blossoms, eight ounces; ravenzara-nuts, one ounce; mace two drachms. Macerate the whole for fifteen days in three and a half gallons of alcohol ; distil, and add to the product a syrup made with ten pounds of sugar. Color with cochineal.

Tabourey Elixir. — Aloes, two drachms ; cinnamon, clove, and nutmeg, each, one ounce ; zests of orange and lemon, each, two. Macerate for fifteen days in five quarts of alcohol, then distil, and add to the product a syrup made cold with six pounds of powdered sugar, two pounds of orange-flower water, and one pound of rose water. Color red.

Elixir of Violets. — Syrup of violets, ten ounces ; filtered raspberry-juice, four ounces ; alcohol, two quarts. Make a syrup with four pounds of sugar, and mix the whole thoroughly.

MISCELLANEOUS LIQUEURS.

Anisette. — Oil of anise-seed, ten drops ; alcohol, three pints ; sugar, two pounds ; pure water, one and a half pounds. Make the syrup with the sugar and water cold, and mix the liquors.

Another Anisette. — Star anise-seed, eight ounces ; bitter almonds pounded, and coriander, each, eight ounces ; powdered Florence iris, four ounces ; alcohol, five gallons. Macerate in the alcohol for five days ; distil in the water-bath, and add twelve pounds of sugar dissolved in seven pints of distilled water.

Anisette de Bourdeaux. — Green anise-seed, ten ounces ; hyson tea, two ounces ; star anise-seed, four ounces ; coriander, one ounce ; fennel, one ounce. Macerate for fifteen days in three and a half gallons of alcohol ; distil in the water-bath ; then make a syrup with ten pounds of sugar and seven pints of water ; mix well, and filter.

Another Anisette de Bourdeaux. — Dill, one pound ; green anise-seed, eight ounces ; fennel, four ounces ; coriander, four ounces ; sassafras-wood cut fine, four ounces ; pearl gunpowder tea, four ounces ; musk-seed, one ounce. Macerate all these substances in three and a half gallons of alcohol for six days; then distil in the water-bath; add a syrup made with twenty-eight pounds of fine sugar, two and a half gallons of distilled water, one quart of double-distilled orange-flower water, and one quart of pure water.

Balm of Mankind. — Peruvian balsam, one ounce; cashew-nuts, eight ounces; coriander, four drachms; dried heads of wormwood, one ounce; yellow rinds of six lemons. Macerate these in two gallons of alcohol for eight days; distil the liquor in the water-bath to nearly one-half; add a syrup made with five and a half pounds of sugar; filter, and color green.

Citronelle. — Zests of lemons, sixty; zests of oranges, eight; nutmeg and cloves, each, one drachm. Macerate the whole in seven quarts of alcohol for fifteen days; distil in the water-bath, and add a syrup made with five pounds of sugar. Color yellow.

Curaçoa. — Surface of the zests of oranges, thirty-six; cinnamon, two drachms; mace, one drachm. Macerate in two gallons of alcohol for fifteen days; distil in the water-bath, and add a syrup made with seven pounds of sugar and two quarts of water. Color with caramel.

Old Men's Milk. — Double-distilled orange-flower water, eight ounces; Peruvian balsam, sixteen drops; alcohol, five quarts. Make a syrup with four pounds of sugar and two pounds of water, and mix with the liquor. This is not colored.

Nectar. — White honey, four ounces; coriander, two ounces; fresh zests of lemon, one ounce; storax calamite, benzoin, and cloves, each, one ounce; tincture of vanilla, half a drachm; tincture of orange-flower water, four ounces; highly rectified spirits, five quarts. Pulverize the substances which require it, and macerate them for fifteen days in the alcohol; then distil the liquor to four quarts in the water bath; add a syrup made with six pounds of fine sugar, with the tincture of vanilla. Color a deep red.

Usquebaugh. — Saffron, one ounce ; dates and nuts without stones and seeds, each, two ounces ; juniper-berries, four drachms ; pounded jujubes, four drachms ; pounded cinnamon, two drachms ; green anise, mace, coriander, and cloves, each, one ounce ; alcohol, four quarts ; syrup boiled to a bead, three quarts. Macerate fifteen days, then strain and add the syrup.

Perfect Love. — Zests of lemon, two ounces ; zests of lime, four ounces ; cloves, two drachms ; alcohol, two and a half gallons ; sugar, ten pounds ; water, five quarts. Macerate ten days in the alcohol ; then distil.

Another Perfect Love. — Lemon zests, two pounds ; cinnamon, half a pound ; rosemary-leaves, quarter of a pound ; orange-flowers, three-eighths of a pound ; pinks, one ounce and a half ; mace, one ounce ; cardamom, one ounce. Macerate in thirty quarts of spirits and fifteen quarts of water ; then distil the liquor to twenty-seven quarts ; add a syrup made of thirty pounds of sugar in thirteen quarts of water, and color with cochineal.

Persicot. — Bitter almonds pounded, ten ounces ; cinnamon, one ounce. Macerate fifteen days in two and a half gallons of alcohol ; distil in the water-bath, and add a syrup made with six pounds of fine sugar. Color with cochineal or caramel.

DOMESTIC WINES.

Currant Wine.— Take ripe currants ; mash them well either with the hands or some broad wooden spoon ; then strain the juice through a strong bag. Have your cask measured, and allow one-third of its contents to be pure juice. As soon as the juice is measured, put it into the cask, which must now be placed in a firm position in the cellar, with spigot provided, so that it may be drawn off without having to move the cask. For every gallon that the cask will hold allow three pounds of brown sugar, and dissolve it in a bucket of water, stirring well; then pour this into the cask, and add more water to the sugar remaining in the bucket until all of it is in the cask; then fill up with water to the bung, and leave it open for *ten* days to ferment. On the tenth day, remove from around the bung-hole all the froth that has collected, using the little finger to reach that inside; then add to a six-gallon cask a half-teacupful of good brandy, and immediately put in the bung pretty tightly. In a day or two, pound it in securely, and let the cask remain undisturbed until the first of January, when it may be quietly racked off, and will be found perfectly clear until the sediment in the bottom is reached. Like all other wine, it improves with age; and although when first drawn it is of a light-red color, it will soon acquire a rich wine tint.

In making all kinds of wine, care must be taken to have the cask perfectly sweet, or the wine will be likely to be sour. If it should smell sour or doubtful, it will be best to have it soaking for a few days beforehand, with a little washing-soda dissolved in the water, rinsing it well before using. Old casks are more desirable than new ones, as, the first time they are used, the wine is likely to taste of the wood.

Blackberry Wine. — This is made precisely as currant wine.

Gooseberry Wine. — Take the fruit when ripe, place it over the fire, with a little water, and let it coddle: this will promote the flow of juice. Keep mashing them with a wooden spoon or masher until the skins are all well softened; then squeeze, and proceed as in currant wine.

Elderberry Wine. — Bruise a bushel of picked elderberries; dilute the mass with *ten* gallons of water, and, having boiled it a few minutes, strain out the juice and squeeze out the husks. Measure the whole, and to every quart put three-quarters of a pound of sugar; then add, while warm, half a pint of yeast, and fill up the cask with some of the reserved liquor: let it ferment for ten days, then cork up. In three months the wine may be drawn off the lees and bottled for use.

Strawberry and Raspberry Wine. — Made like currant wine.

Rhubarb Wine. — Take the large juicy stalks of the rhubarb, or pie-plant, cut them up into pieces about an inch long, cover them with water, and stew them until perfectly soft; then cool them, and strain the juice; after which, proceed as for currant wine.

CHAPTER XXII.

JELLIES, MARMALADES, PRESERVES.

GELATINE. — CALVES'-FOOT JELLY. — CALVES'-FOOT JELLY FROM PREPARED GELATINE — BLANCMANGE.— QUINCE JELLY. — CURRANT JELLY. — CURRANT AND RASPBERRY JELLY. — RASPBERRY JELLY. — GRAPE JELLY. — STRAWBERRY AND BLACKBERRY JELLIES. — APPLE JELLY. — CHERRY JELLY. — ORANGE-PASTE. — APRICOT JELLY. — QUINCE BREAD. — QUINCE SALMON.— QUINCE-PASTE.— APPLE-PULP.— QUINCE-JUICE.— QUINCE SNOW. — SWEET ORANGE JELLY. — DRIED ORANGE-PEEL. — LEMON JELLY. — STRAWBERRY-PASTE. — JELLY WITH SALEP. — RED OR BLACK CURRANT PASTE. — TO PRESERVE CURRANT-JUICE.

GELATINE.

THIS is a substance which is found in all animal bodies, especially in the tendons, ligaments, cellular membranes; and forms the framework of the bones themselves. When the parts containing it are boiled for several hours, the water on cooling will be found in the form of a firm jelly, which can be again melted by heat. The substance known as *isinglass* is the gelatine obtained from certain fishes. The refined gelatine used for table jelly is transparent, and almost colorless and tasteless.

CALVES'-FOOT JELLY.

Soak four fresh calves' feet in water until the blood is entirely washed out; then put them into an ordinary iron pot or saucepan with a gallon of water; let them boil until they are completely boiled to shreds, and the water is half gone; take them from the fire, and pour the whole through a tin strainer so as to keep out all the pieces of bones and flesh; then set the bowl containing the liquor in a cool place until it becomes quite solid. Before removing it from the vessel in which it cooled, scrape off carefully all the grease from the top, which may be done first with a spoon, and afterwards with a knife : when all has been taken off in that way, a towel may be laid on, and thus all remaining fatty particles will be taken up. Now have ready a preserving kettle, and turn into it the solid cake of gelatine, and set it in a place near the stove, or where it will melt gradually, while you are preparing the materials for clarifying and flavoring. Take the whites of six eggs well beaten, and add to the gelatine, together with the egg-shells, as soon as it is entirely liquefied; then set it where it will boil. If the lump of gelatine is as solid as cheese, it will be better to add a pint of water also. Now squeeze the juice of three lemons, and grate the rinds, pouring a little boiling water on the latter, which will help to extract both the coloring and flavor of the rind ; have this ready to add with the wine and sugar at the last. When the jelly is clear, it can be seen boiling up in the middle ; and, by holding in a silver spoon, it will show the clear liquid separated from the froth and scum. The scum should now be removed, and, after that, the flavoring and sugar added to suit the taste ; then the whole poured through a flannel bag, being very careful not to squeeze it at all : generally it runs through perfectly clear at first, but may require a second straining. After it is strained, add Madeira or sherry wine to the taste, stir it well, and pour into dishes or moulds to cool.

CALVES'-FOOT JELLY MADE OF PREPARED GELATINE.

Take one package of Cox's gelatine, add to it a pint and a half of cold water, and let it stand an hour. Grate the rinds of three lemons, and pour on a small quantity of boiling water, then squeeze the juice. When the gelatine has steeped an hour, add the juice, and pour off the water from the grated rinds; then add to the whole a pint and a half of boiling water, stirring well. Now sweeten it to the taste,

Blancmange. — Jellies.

and add wine also to suit, with a few drops of orange-flower water. Then set it away in moulds or dishes to cool, without straining or cooking. In a few hours, you will have nearly two quarts of clear, sparkling jelly.

BLANCMANGE.

Take one package of Cox's gelatine, and put it to steep as above, only using $1\frac{1}{2}$ pint of milk; then add $1\frac{1}{2}$ pint of boiling milk or cream, and sweeten to the taste: when it is nearly cool, add wine to the taste, also a few drops of almond extract. A good flavor is also obtained by boiling in the milk a few peach-leaves; this will take the place of bitter almonds, as a flavor: pour into moulds, and set in a cold place.

QUINCE JELLY.

Quarter and core half a peck of ripe quinces, cover them with water, and boil them until they are well done, which may be determined by running a fork through them. Strain the liquor through a flannel bag, and measure it, allowing one pound of white sugar to each pint of juice: place the whole on the fire in a preserving kettle, and watch it closely lest it boil over. Try it occasionally on a saucer; and when it begins to jelly, or grow solid, it is done.

CURRANT JELLY.

Squeeze the currants (fully ripe), and to every pint of juice add one pound fine white sugar. Let it boil twenty minutes, scumming it while on the fire. Do not let it remain longer than this, or it will become dark: pour it immediately into cups and glasses.

ANOTHER MODE.

Measure the currant-juice, allowing, as above, a pound of sugar to every pint of juice, but do not mix them; place the juice on the fire; boil and scum it for twenty minutes; have the sugar in a large pitcher, and pour the hot juice on to it, stirring it briskly until all is dissolved; then fill up your jars as quickly as possible, as it will jelly immediately. Jelly made in this way is lighter colored than when the sugar is boiled, and by most persons it is therefore preferred.

CURRANT AND RASPBERRY JELLY.

Take equal quantities of currants and raspberries, strain the juice, and proceed as with others, always allowing one pound of sugar to a pint of juice.

RASPBERRY JELLY.

Squeeze the fruit through the flannel bag, and proceed as above.

GRAPE JELLY.

Choose fine ripe grapes; place them in a preserving kettle over a moderate fire, with a little water to prevent their burning; when they are hot enough to burst the skins, the juice may easily be pressed out, and strained through the bag: proceed as before.

STRAWBERRY AND BLACKBERRY JELLY.

Both are made precisely as raspberry jelly.

APPLE JELLY.

Take pippins, or other tart apples, cut them in quarters, pare and core them; place them in a preserving kettle covered with water, and let them boil to a marmalade. Now strain the juice without squeezing through a clean jelly bag, and for every pint of juice add one pound of fine sugar. The rind of one or two lemons boiled with the apples improves the flavor; and if the apples are not very tart, add the juice also.

CHERRY JELLY.

Take ripe sour cherries, and place in a preserving kettle; then set it over the fire until the heat causes the juice to flow freely; strain and proceed as with grape jelly.

ORANGE PASTE.

Prepare the oranges as for the marmalade, only it must be heated or dried longer. When it has boiled up several times, put it on a flat surface in small, round cakes, and let it dry. Cut the cakes with a thin knife which has been dipped in warm water, and press two of the same size together; put them up in little boxes or jars.

SMALL GREEN ORANGES PRESERVED WHOLE.

Pierce small, green oranges several times with a knife, and boil them very soft; let them stand three days in water, which must be poured on every day fresh; put them again in a dish, pour over them thin clarified sugar, and proceed as with the orange-peel in the receipt for bitter oranges. Small green lemons are preserved in the same manner. They are commonly glazed or candied.

APRICOT JELLY.

Choose apricots that are just ripe; pare, and cut them in two, and take out the stones; boil them in a sufficient quantity of water, strain through a hair sieve, and pour the decoction into earthen dishes; then for every pint of liquid take a pound of sugar, and finish the operation like currant jelly. This jelly has an exquisite taste, especially when a few pieces of preserved orange are added; after the jelly has been boiled, cherry-juice is prepared like the currant-juice, or in the following way: —

When the juice is pressed out, put it in glass bottles, put in one pound of powdered-sugar to one pound of juice, a little cinnamon and sugar; then shake the bottles until the sugar is melted; let it stand eight days, filter the juice, pour it again into bottles, fasten them, and keep them in a cool place.

QUINCE BREAD.

Rub off the down from the quinces with a cloth, cut out the blossoms, pare them, and boil them very soft; scrape off the pulp, weigh it, and to every pound put one pound of dry sugar; stir it well, and boil it by a good fire, stirring it constantly. When it is almost done, put in some powdered cinnamon and cloves, then lemon and orange-peel. When it no longer adheres to the side of the kettle, it is done. Spread it out in the dish to stand in a dry, warm room, and the next day put it into boxes between paper.

QUINCE SALMON.

When the quinces have been rubbed and cut as in the last receipt, and boiled not quite so soft, pare them, and cut them in small pieces. Take to every pound of the prepared quince one pound of clarified sugar; boil it, stirring all the time, by a slow fire till it becomes red; then put it into forms, generally of fish, and prepared like the quince bread.

QUINCE PASTE.

Clean, cook, pare, and scrape the quinces. Warm the pulp, boil to a flake equal weights of sugar, and boil both for some time. Put it on plates or in boxes, and cut it in long, square pieces.

APPLE PULP.

Boil the apples as in the marmalade, or take what remains from the jelly and press it through the sieve. Warm the pulp, dry it, and boil to a flake equal weights of sugar, and let them boil together by a gentle fire. Put the pulp about half-inch deep in paper boxes. When it is dry enough, take it out of the box, and cut the apple in long or square strips.

QUINCE JUICE.

Boil and press the quinces, as in the jelly; put to a pint of juice one pound of finely powdered sugar, let it boil up once, skim it, and put it into bottles.

This may be colored by boiling in the juice some oil of orange-flowers.

QUINCE SNOW.

Boil to a flake one pound of sugar, warm half a pound of quince pulp, stir in the sugar, and let it warm again. Beat up the whites of three eggs, stir it in the mixture, and put it on a plate, ornamented with quince bread or quince salmon.

SWEET ORANGE JELLY.

Take ripe, soft apples, cut them in thin slices, pour over some water, and let them boil tender. During the boiling, press the apples so that the juice runs out, put them on a hair-sieve, and let the juice drain off. To one pint of juice put three-quarters of a pound of refined sugar in which the peels of two oranges have been grated. Boil until the syrup runs thick and broad from the spoon; then squeeze in the two oranges, let all boil up once more, and put into jars.

DRIED ORANGE-PEEL.

Boil refined sugar to a small flake, put in preserved orange-peel from which the sugar has drained, boil the sugar to a large flake, stir it often lest it should burn, take it off and put it on a slab: stir the peel until the ebullition subsides, then take out the orange-peel, put it on a wire sieve, and let it cool.

LEMON JELLY.

Grate three or four lemons into fine refined sugar, and press out the juice; boil three-fourths of an ounce of isinglass with one quart of water till it is boiled to one-half the quantity. Put in the juice, sweeten to the taste with refined sugar, let it become very hot on a coal fire, then pour it into a glass or porcelain dish, and let it jellify in a cool place.

STRAWBERRY-PASTE.

This is like the currant-paste, except that a pound and a half of sugar is used to one pound of pulp; half a pound of apple-pulp may be mixed with one pound of the strawberry marmalade, and the sugar added.

JELLY WITH SALEP.

Put a quarter of an ounce of pulverized salep into a kettle with a pint of water, the peel of a lemon, and a quarter of a pound of sugar; boil the whole together a quarter of an hour, add the juice of the peeled lemons, and strain through a cloth: this is very pleasant and cooling for sick persons.

RED OR BLACK CURRANT PASTE.

Take off the stems, put the berries into a vessel placed in boiling water, let them stay twenty or thirty minutes, then pass them through a hair sieve; heat this pulp by a gentle fire, and stir into it, for every pound, a pound of powdered sugar; stir it till it boils up once, then proceed as in the last.

MEANS FOR PRESERVING CURRANT-JUICE A YEAR.

Currants, 4 lbs.; raspberries, 1 lb.

Choose the fruit before it is quite ripe; having stemmed the currants, and hulled the raspberries, squeeze them through a cloth, and pour the juice into glass bottles, sealing the cork. Immerse the bottles to the neck in cold water, in a kettle surrounded by hay; place the kettle on the fire, and take it off after two or three boilings: when the water is cold, take out the bottles, and put them away in a cellar. This method preserves the taste, acidity, and quality of the currants. The bottles must be entirely filled.

CHAPTER XXIII.

BRANDY FRUITS.

PREPARATION OF BRANDY FRUITS. — PEACHES IN BRANDY. — APRICOTS IN BRANDY. — GREENGAGES IN BRANDY. — PLUMS IN BRANDY. — PEARS IN BRANDY. — CHERRIES IN BRANDY. — BELGIAN MODE OF BRANDYING CHERRIES. — BRANDY ORANGES. — BRANDY GRAPES. — BRANDY PEARS (ANOTHER RULE). — BRANDY QUINCES. — BRANDY MELON RINDS. — CHINESE BRANDY FRUITS.

PREPARATION OF BRANDY FRUITS.

FOR these fruits to be perfect it is necessary, 1st, To gather them at the proper degree of maturity; 2d, To perform carefully all the preliminary operations; 3d, To follow such rules as will destroy their natural characteristics as little as possible, and will insure their preservation. We will examine these three principal points: —

All fruits that possess a certain firmness, and the more fleshy kinds of vegetables, may be preserved in brandy; but stoned fruits are the most frequently prepared, and also some species of pears, quince, green lemons, some kinds of grapes, melon and lime rinds, and all fruits capable of yielding useful and pleasant flavorings. These preparations do not aim at preserving the fruits in their natural condition, but at transforming them into more delicate dishes.

The fruits destined for brandy-preserves should be healthy and pulpy. They are gathered just before their perfect maturity, that they may preserve a certain degree of firmness: this precaution is especially necessary if their nature be soft and yielding. Those which are gathered perfectly ripe are too pulpy, and could not support a certain degree of heat, or long maceration in water, without losing their form, and falling in marmalade, even before being sufficiently impregnated with the sugar and alcohol; and, instead of their own juice, they become penetrated with brandy, and thus are spongy, and possess little delicacy of flavor.

Merchants who deal in large quantities of brandy-fruits prepare beforehand a mixture of two parts of brandy to one of good sugar-syrup well clarified: they filter it, and keep it on hand for use. As the season for the different fruits arrives, they blanche them, put them into jars, fill up the jars with the sugared brandy, and let the fruits stand for two or three months, or even longer, according to their size. Fruits prepared in this manner, being less penetrated with the sugar, and not too much so with brandy, are preferred by many people: they have the advantage of being less soft than, and nearly as beautifully colored as, when they were gathered; the liquor itself is as limpid as possible, which circumstance flatters the eye as well as the taste.

Whatever process is followed, the aroma of the fruit is dissolved in the brandy, and, as it lies principally in the skin, it is best not to peel the fruits. Again: the fruit gives up more or less easily a portion of its juice in order to draw in the brandy; so that, if it imbibes to the core the liquid in which it is bathed, that will combine with the juice, and produce a genuine ratafia. This exchange is more prompt and complete when the brandy is not saturated with sugar: it may be remarked in this case that the liquor has almost entirely drained the fruit, which, on its side, is filled with brandy. This perfectly accords with what is said in the article on ratafias, and explains the reason that sugar must only be added after the maceration of those substances whose flavor and perfume we wish to extract; while, in the preparation of brandy-fruits, we soften the strength of this liquor with sugar before submitting the fruits to its action. We should recommend to those who aim at perfection to employ, instead of brandy, spirits of wine mixed with the juice of the fruits. No just proportions can be assigned for the fruit sugar and brandy, nor the strength of the latter. It is enough to know that the fruit must be completely covered with the liquor; that, in general, from four to six ounces of sugar are used for every quart of brandy: but it can be easily seen that these rules are very variable; the strength of the brandy, and the proportion of the sugar, must be augmented or diminished according to the sweetness of the fruit. If its juice were not sufficiently saturated with the sugar and brandy, it would soon ferment. But fruits well prepared can be kept in this state for a year or two; but, even if they begin to ferment, the continued maceration would soften them, and end by reducing them to a marmalade. The jars should be tightly covered, filled quite full, and kept in a place rather cool. The fruit does not keep so well in large jars as in small, since fermentation commences sooner in them.

PEACHES IN BRANDY.

Peaches, and indeed all large fruit intended to be preserved in brandy, must first be prepared as for compotes; with this difference, that the fruit should be barely half done through. As one of the first qualifications to perfection in fruits preserved in brandy arises from their retaining as much as possible their original color, in order to attain that end, it is essential that none but perfect fruit be selected for the purpose. Further, every care and precaution must be taken to insure cleanliness and strict attention throughout the operation; for otherwise you cannot hope to succeed, and the result of your expense and labor will tend only to produce dark, hard, unsightly fruits not worth eating. When the peaches have been split in halves, scalded in syrup, and their skins removed, let them simmer very gently for not more than five minutes in the same syrup in which they were scalded, and set them aside in a pan with their syrup until the next day : the peaches are then to be carefully and neatly placed and arranged in wide-mouthed bottles, or rather jars ; their syrup is to be boiled down to the consistency of sugar at the feather degree, and an equal proportion of *very* pale or white brandy added to this, and allowed to become *nearly* cold before it is poured in upon the peaches : when *thoroughly* cold, they must be well corked down, covered in with bladder, and kept in a cool temperature.

APRICOTS IN BRANDY.

These are prepared in the same way as peaches, excepting that the apricots are to be thinly peeled instead of skinned ; indeed, it is more customary to preserve them whole, without either skinning or peeling them.

GREENGAGES IN BRANDY.

Prepare these in the first instance as directed on p. 160, bearing in mind that they must only be half done through ; their syrup is then to be boiled down and mixed with an equal proportion of pale brandy previously to their being finished off.

PLUMS IN BRANDY.

The same as greengages, leaving out the greening process.

PEARS IN BRANDY.

Divide the pears in halves or quarters, and as they are turned out of hand drop them into some acidulated water, to prevent them from becoming brown ; then let the pieces of pear simmer in syrup till half done through, and finish them as directed for peaches.

CHERRIES IN BRANDY.

Morello cherries are fittest for this purpose ; cut the stalks off to within half an inch of the fruit, and, as you do so, drop each cherry into a glass jar; when the jars are all complete and ready to receive the liquid, mix equal proportions of twenty-eight degrees syrup, cold, and brandy, and pour this to the cherries; cork them down tight, tie them over with bladder, and keep the jars in a cool temperature.

BELGIAN METHOD OF BRANDY CHERRIES.

Take early cherries, perfectly ripe, break them off the stem, pound them and break the stones; put them with sugar in a kettle, and boil them until half the syrup is boiled away; pour this boiling compound in brandy to which have been added the desired spices, and let the mixture stand in the sun. When the season for raspberries is come, some of them can be added if thought fit. This is done in the following manner: At a month after the season of early cherries, the late kind ripen, and these are to be crushed, pressed through a cloth, and filtered, and then made into a ratafia with raspberries; then with this the first cherries are mixed, and thus preserve their volume and color, and have a much finer taste. The following is the proportion of the divers ingredients: early cherries, 6 lbs.; raspberries, 1 lb.; sugar, 3 lbs.; brandy, 5 quarts; pink-petals, à ratafia; 6 oz. of ratafia of cloves may be substituted for the pink, or 2 drams of cinnamon or vanilla in powder.

BRANDY ORANGES.

Of all fruits which are at our disposal, the orange is one of those whose flavor is the most agreeable; the Maltese is a very fine variety, and the Portugal is the finest of all. Strip the oranges of their rind, puncture them, and throw them into fresh water; then, having blanched them over a moderate fire, plunge them again in the cold water; liquefy a sufficient quantity of sugar, and boil it to syrup to be poured over the oranges, placed in a kettle and boiled till the surface is covered with bubbles, then removed and allowed to stand for twenty-four hours, and boiled to the same point again, removed and again boiled, and the third time drained off to be put into jars. When these operations are finished, put the syrup on the fire again, and let it boil a few minutes; when cold, add two parts of brandy, and mix it thoroughly; filter through a cloth, and pour it over the fruit until it is entirely covered; close the jars as tightly as possible to preserve them, taking the precautions already mentioned for the others.

BRANDY GRAPES.

Break off the grapes from the stem, and throw them one by one, without bruising them, in a vessel full of fresh water, and pierce them in two or three places with a pin; then express the juice of some other grapes, and mix with brandy. Drain off the washed grapes, and dry them with a fine cloth; put them in jars, which are to be filled with the mixture of brandy and grape juice, to which has been added the necessary quantity of sugar or syrup. If any flavor is wanted besides that of the grapes, any one can be used at pleasure.

BRANDY PEARS, ANOTHER RULE.

Choose fine pears, with short stems remaining on them; they may either be pared or not, according to taste; if pared, they must be done carefully, and as thin a coat as possible removed; place them at once in the jars, and pour over them finely powdered sugar, about one-third of a pound to a pound of fruit: set the jars in a kettle of cold water, and place this over the fire, allowing the water to boil around them; when the jars are nearly half filled with syrup, remove the kettle, and let them cool in the water; then, when the fruit is cold, fill up the jars with white brandy, shake gently so as to mix well, cork and set in a cool place. This plan of preparing brandy fruits is far less trouble than those already given, although some prefer the first. This plan has this additional advantage : the beauty of brandied fruit consists in their preserving their natural shape, and the less handling they have the better ; thus, by placing them at once in the jars, all further handling is avoided. The other fruits may all be prepared in the same manner.

BRANDY QUINCES.

These, being a very hard fruit, require to be boiled until tender in water, then taken out and well drained. Now place on the fire with your sugar, and let them simmer until the syrup has had time to penetrate the fruit, say fifteen minutes, when they may be taken off and placed in the jars, dividing the syrup among them; when cool, fill up with brandy, and cork.

BRANDY MELON-RINDS.

All the melons fit to eat can be preserved in brandy. Having cut away the juicy part of the melon, and the superficial part of the rind, cut the rind in square pieces, and throw them into a basin containing some cold water and some lemon-juice ; place the basin on the fire for two or three boilings ; let it stew for an hour ; then throw the pieces of melon in some other water with lemon-juice to cool, and treat them exactly like the quarters of quince, taking care to put in the syrup a little fresh angelica, and some fresh ginger-root, or essence of lemon.

CHINESE BRANDY FRUITS.

This name is given to a preserve of little green lemons. Choose either unripe lemons or oranges, prick them in two or three places with a pin, and throw them into a kettle containing water, and several handfuls of ashes enclosed in a cloth ; place the whole on the fire, and let it boil a few minutes ; then diminish the fire to prolong the infusion, without giving the fruits time to boil ; then throw them into a bucket.

CHAPTER XXIV

MARMALADES OR JAMS.—CONSERVES.

WHAT MARMALADES ARE.—PEACH OR APRICOT MARMALADES.—CHERRY JAM.—MARMALADE OF ORANGE AND LEMON PEEL.—GREENGAGE MARMALADE.—ORANGE MARMALADE.—PINE-APPLE MARMALADE.—STRAWBERRY OR RASPBERRY JAM.—QUINCE MARMALADE.—PEAR MARMALADE.—FRUIT CONSERVES.—WORMWOOD CONSERVES.—ORANGE-FLOWER AND ROSE CONSERVES.—VIOLET CONSERVE.—JELLY OF FRUIT-JUICE.

MARMALADES OR JAMS

ARE mixtures of fruits and sugar reduced to a paste of suitable consistence for preserving. Ripe fruits are employed for this purpose, which could not support the blanching process necessary for entire comfitures. The beauty of marmalades depends on the fruits employed and the quality of the sugar, on the boiling, and the care bestowed on the whole operation.

To procure a fine marmalade, choose ripe, luscious fruits, cut them into small pieces, and, adding the sugar in layers, with a layer of fruit always on the bottom of the preserving kettle, set it over the fire; if the fruit is not very juicy, it will be best to add a small portion of water. As the fruit boils, shake the kettle occasionally by lifting it from the fire, and turning the whole briskly to prevent its burning at the bottom: it should not be stirred with a spoon, as that is almost sure to make it burn. When the whole begins to look clear, and grows thick upon cooling a portion on a plate, it is done, and may be taken from the fire and put into jars at once.

PEACH OR APRICOT MARMALADES.

Take ripe fruit of either kind, pare and cut them up in small pieces, place them in a preserving kettle, with a layer of fruit in the bottom, then a layer of sugar, so alternating until all is in ; allow three-fourths of a pound of sugar for each pound of fruit; then cook them over the fire, watching them carefully that they may not burn.

CHERRY JAM.

Choose fine ripe cherries, stone them, being careful not to lose the juice. To every pound of fruit take three-fourths of a pound of sugar; place them on the fire and boil until the syrup is clear and will jellify upon cooling a portion on a plate.

MARMALADE OF ORANGE AND LEMON PEEL.

Put a number of rinds into a jar of water, and let them soak for several days ; then drain them, and pound or mash them soft, adding a small quantity of water, with one-half a pound of sugar to every pound of pulp ; cook about three-fourths of an hour.

GREENGAGE PLUM MARMALADE.

Plums very green and ripe, 12 lbs.; clarified sugar, 9 lbs.

Proceed as with the apricot marmalade, only adding a small quantity of water when first put on the fire. In the same way, and with like proportions, all plum marmalades are made.

ORANGE MARMALADE.

Take fine oranges, remove the rind and grate the pulp, preserving carefully the juice and taking out seeds ; add to every six oranges the juice and grated rind of two lemons ; weigh the whole, and allow for every pound three-fourths of a pound of sugar ; cook the whole, adding the grated rind of the oranges ; when done, it will be quite thick and solid.

PINE-APPLE MARMALADE.

Pare the fruit, and remove the pines; then grate the pineapple, preserving the juice; allow three-fourths of a pound of sugar to each pound of grated fruit.

STRAWBERRY OR RASPBERRY JAM.

Take ripe fruit and weigh them, allowing equal weights of sugar and fruit; when they will jellify on cooling, they are done. Raspberry jam is improved by the addition of a little currant-juice, all being cooked together.

QUINCE MARMALADE.

Take ripe quinces, pare and cut them in small pieces, stew them in sufficient water to cover them until they can be mashed with a wooden spoon; when well mashed up in the water, put in the sugar (having weighed the fruit before beginning to cook it), allowing three-fourths of a pound of sugar to one pound of fruit; as it cooks it will assume a bright red color, and will be quite thick and solid when cold.

PEAR MARMALADE.

Peel the pears, quarter them, and take out the seeds; throw them into a little fresh water, and place them on the fire; when they are sufficiently soft, mash them with a wooden spoon; then add the sugar with the juice and grated rinds of several lemons; mix well, and replace the whole on the fire; stir it while boiling until it is of sufficient consistency, then pour it into pots: in the same way, apple marmalade can be made. For both, the following proportions are required: fruits, $3\frac{1}{2}$ lbs.; sugar, 2 lbs.

There yet remains for our notice the kind of marmalades called Fruit Conserves. In these the fruit is not preserved whole, as in compotes, but made into a paste; thus:—

WORMWOOD CONSERVE.

Heads of wormwood in powder, 4 drams; powdered sugar, 1 lb.

Mix the powders, and make of them a paste with distilled wormwood water. It is a good stomachic.

ORANGE-FLOWER AND ROSE CONSERVES

Are made by steeping the petals in distilled water, adding the sugar, and heating it over a moderate fire: the proportions are powdered petals, 4 oz.; sugar, 1½ lb.; orange-flower or rose-water, 8 oz.

VIOLET CONSERVE

Is made with a pound of fresh violet petals, powdered with care, and mixed in the sugar boiled to a flake.

JELLY OF FRUIT-JUICE.

Boil grape-juice for an hour, if it has not been cooked, and add one part of farina to ten parts of juice. This tastes something like currant jelly.

CHAPTER XXV

COMPOTES.

Apple Compotes. — Compote of Whole Apples. — Stuffed Apple Compote. — Compote of Apples Grillés. — Compote of Apple-Paste. — Compote of Apples à la Duchesse. — Compote of Apple Jelly. — Compote of Apples à la Cintra. — Compote of Apple Marmalade. — Compote of Pears, White. — Compote of Pears, Pink. — Compote of Pears à la Princesse. — Compote of Pears à la Victoria. — Compote of Pears Variegated. — Compote of Pears à la Zingara. — Compote of Oranges. — Compote of Oranges à l'Espagnole. — Apricot Compote. — Chestnut Compote. — Chestnut Compote with Cream. — Strawberry Compote. — Green Gooseberry Compote. — Cherry Compote. — Peach Compote. — Another Pear Compote. — Compote of Roast Pears. — Grape Compote. — Salade d'Oranges. — Compote of Orange Baskets filled with Fruits. — Compote of Lemon Baskets. — Compote of Cherries. — Compote of Currants. — Compote of Currants in Bunches. — Compote of Plums. — Compote of Apricots. — Compote of Greengages. — Compote of Pomegranates. — Compote of Arlequinade. — Compote of Green Figs. — Another Compote of Peaches. — Compote of Peaches Grillés. — Another Compote of Pine-Apple. — Compote of Whole Oranges. — Compote of Whole Lemons. — Compote of Imitation Ginger. — Compote of Chestnuts Glacés. — Compote of Chestnut Paste. — Compote of Vermacellied Chestnuts. — Compote of Green Walnuts. — Compote of Green Filberts. — Compote of Barberries. — Compote of Crab-Apples. — Compote of Cranberries. — Compote of Grapes. — Compote of Dried Normandy Pippins. — Compote of Cocoanut, White. — Compote of Cocoanut, Pink. — Compote of Dried Fruits in Apple Jelly. — Compote of Spanish Branco. — Compote of Sandwiches à la Sevillane. — Compote à la Ximenes. — Compote of Spanish Vermicelli. — Prune Compote. — Pine-Apple Compote. — Diplomatic Apple Compote. — Portuguese Compote. — Diversified Compote.

These are fruits preserved with very little sugar, and made as they are needed; the fruits are blanched, a little sugar added for them to absorb, and then they are put in dishes, and the syrup poured over them; for the sake of appearance (for which so much labor is everywhere expended), they are ornamented in divers ways with preserved fruits and jellies, and covered with jelly: great care should be taken to preserve the form and whiteness of the fruits and syrups. For this purpose, when you peel apples, pears, &c., rub them immediately with a cut lemon, and squeeze a little lemon-juice into the syrup. In peeling the fruits, they may be cut into many fanciful shapes, and, to obliterate the traces of the knife, the blade passed down over its marks; the fruit may be blanched either in water or thinned syrup. The first method is the most economical, and the fruit does not need so much sugar; but the second produces the better compotes. To preserve the whiteness of the peeled fruits, they should be peeled as rapidly as possible, put into a saucepan with the water or syrup, blanched only long enough to soften, ranged in the dish, and covered with syrup. To remove the skin from peaches, apricots, apples, &c., you may throw them into boiling water, and let them boil up once or twice, after which the skin will come off easily: if the fruits are not ripe, they ought to be put in syrup over the fire to correct their crudity.

APPLE COMPOTE.

Cut and boil the apples, drain off the juice, sweeten it with refined sugar, and put in the finely cut peel of a lemon, together with the juice. Pare any kind of good apples, cut them in quarters, take out the core, pierce them several times, and let them boil soft in the juice, but not pithy; take them out, lay them to drain, and, when cold, put them in compote dishes. Drain off the juice and boil it to a jelly, skim it well, pour it about the thickness of a quill on a plate, or on as many plates as there are compote dishes; the plates must be dipped first in cold water; pour some jelly on the apples. When the jelly on the plates is stiff, warm them slightly, and with a knife take them off, and place them over the apples in the compote dishes: this is very good.

ANOTHER COMPOTE OF APPLES.

Cut the apples in halves, scoop out the cores neatly, either turn or peel them in straight bands of equal breadths, and, as each is turned out of hand, drop it into some acidulated water; simmer in twenty-eight degrees syrup until the apples are partially done through, and allow them to steep in their syrup in a basin until they are dished up; they must have been well-drained on a napkin; decorate the compote with angelica, the red peel of apples, and different sorts of preserve, all previously cut in thin sheets or slices, and stamped out with tin cutters in ornamental shapes to form tasteful designs upon each piece of apple, representing wreaths, stars, &c.: cover the whole with a thin sheet of apple-jelly.

COMPOTE OF WHOLE APPLES.

First, remove the core in its whole length by inserting a long tin cutter (tapering at one end) at each end of the apple, and with the point of the index finger force out the core; by using this precaution, you will not split the apple; place the apples in acidulated water to keep them white as they are turned spirally out of hand. Finish the compote as directed in the foregoing case.

STUFFED APPLE COMPOTE.

Pare fine large apples, take out the core, leaving the apples entire, fill the opening with apricot or orange marmalade, put them near together in a saucepan, pour over them clarified sugar, and cook them soft in the oven.

COMPOTE OF APPLES GRILLÉS.

A compote is said to be *grillé* when it has undergone the following process: When it happens that you have the remains of compotes of apples or pears having lost their original whiteness, put them in a flat pan, or a sautapan for instance, and set the pan over a brisk fire, that the accompanying syrup may be boiled down quickly to a light-colored caramel; use a fork to roll gently and carefully each piece of apple in the caramelled syrup, in order that the rounded part may present an even, glossy surface; and, as they are thus glazed out of hand, let them be dished up at once in their compotier; just before sending to table, pour a little curaçoa round the base of the fruit.

COMPOTE OF APPLE-PASTE.

Reduce sufficient marmalade of apples to serve your purpose; color one-half pink with a few drops of cochineal, and spread each lot about half an inch thick upon clean plates, and set them aside to become stiff and cold. When cold, cut out the marmalade, with a knife or with a tin cutter, in squares, diamonds, rings, ovals, leaves, &c.; use a fork to dip each of these in some caramelled syrup; and as each piece is so dipped, place it out of hand upon a trellised wire drainer resting on a dish; and, when all are complete, put them in the screen to dry for twenty minutes; dish up this compote pyramidally, and pour a little cinnamon liqueur round the base.

COMPOTE OF APPLES À LA DUCHESSE.

For this compote choose golden pippins of equal size, and free from blemish; remove the cores, turn them, and when they are three parts done in syrup, drain them upon a baking sheet, and finish them by baking them for a few minutes in a rather sharp oven; and when they are withdrawn, and while hot, fill up the interiors with apricot jam, and use a fork to roll each apple in jelly produced by boiling down the syrup used to dress it in; this will give the apples a beautiful gloss. Dish up the compote in a pyramidal form, imitate the stalks with a piece of green angelica, and pour a little maraschino round the base.

COMPOTE OF APPLE JELLY.

Prepare some apple jelly; and, when ready, pour it into small moulds; when the jelly is set firm, these are to be turned out in symmetrical order in their compotier, and decorated with other colored preserves, or with green angelica.

COMPOTE OF APPLES À LA CINTRA.

Cut the apples in thick slices, stamp out the cores, remove the peel, and turn the edges smooth; let the apples simmer in syrup. Cut three oranges in slices, pick out the pips, remove the rind bare to the pulp of the fruit, and immerse in boiling syrup, merely to steep for an hour or so, away from the fire. When about to dish up the compote, drain the oranges and apples on a napkin, cover the pieces of orange on one side only with a thin layer of apricot jam, and the pieces of apple in a similar manner with red-currant jelly; dish them up by placing a slice of orange and a slice of apple alternately in the compotier, and raise the compote in three tiers of slices so placed; ornament with green angelica, and pour some syrup flavored with rum round the base.

COMPOTE OF APPLE MARMALADE.

Prepare some apple marmalade with ribston pippins; and, when ready, pour it into a small jelly mould, or some smaller moulds, seven in number, and let them be slightly oiled inside with oil of almonds; when set firm by becoming cold, the marmalade is to be turned out and placed in the compotier; pour some orange syrup round the base.

COMPOTE OF PEARS, WHITE.

Every kind of fine-flavored dessert pears suit this purpose; divide the fruit in halves or quarters, according to the size of the pears used for making the compote; remove the cores, pare and trim the pieces neatly, simmer them in slightly acidulated syrup, keeping them firm to the touch; dish up the pieces in close order, decorate the compote in the usual manner, and cover it with a sheet of apple jelly; pour some of the syrup round the base.

COMPOTE OF PEARS, PINK.

This is prepared in exactly the same manner as the foregoing; the only difference being, in order to give a very light pink tinge of color to the pears, a few drops of prepared cochineal should be added to the syrup in which the pears are to simmer; decorate the compote with angelica.

COMPOTE OF PEARS, À LA PRINCESSE.

Select seven pears of best quality and of equal size, scrape the stalks, and turn them spirally from head to stalk; let the pears simmer in syrup containing a little lemon-juice to keep them as white as possible, and when done, and steeped some time in their syrup, cut off the pointed ends of the fruit, so as to leave the stalk ends measuring about half an inch surface in diameter; upon each place a similar sized ring of angelica; upon this set a large strawberry or stoned cherry (either must be passed through hot syrup), and run a strip of angelica through all to imitate the stalks of the pears; when dished up, pour some syrup over the compote.

COMPOTE OF PEARS, À LA VICTORIA.

In this case also seven pears are required; trim and remove the cores through the thick end half-way down the fruit, previously to its being turned spirally, in order not to split or in any way damage the shape of the pears; let them simmer in very light pink syrup merely to give them a delicate tinge of color; and when they are done, let them be drained on a napkin, fill their interiors with fresh strawberry jam, decorate them as in the preceding case, using mirabelle plums instead of cherries. When dished up, the pears must* be placed in the compotier in an upright position to give due effect to the decoration; pour some of the syrup flavored with vanilla round the base.

COMPOTE OF PEARS VARIEGATED.

This has a charming appearance; the remains of the two former compotes may serve the purpose by your placing a white and a pink pear alternately in the compotier; finish in the same manner.

COMPOTE OF PEARS À LA ZINGARA.

Prepare some thick slices of pears, which, after being simmered in syrup in the usual manner, are to be *glacés* in their own syrup, similarly to compote of apples *grillés*. Prepare also some slices of oranges as in Compote of Apples à la Cintra. When about to dish up the compote, place the pieces of pears and oranges alternately resting upon each other in the same manner as cutlets are dished up; build up the compote three tiers in elevation, decorate it with angelica upon the pieces of oranges, and with damson cheese or currant jelly upon the bright brown glossy pieces of pears. Pour some syrup flavored with Dantzic brandy round the base.

COMPOTE OF ORANGES.

Divide six oranges in halves; first cut out the centre string of pith, pick out all the pips carefully, and with a very sharp knife *pare* off the *peel* of the oranges by cutting *through* to the transparent, naked pulp of the fruit; place the halves as they are turned out of hand in a basin, and, when all are completed, pour over them some hot twenty-eight degrees syrup, flavored with some of the rind rubbed on pieces of lump sugar and previously infused in the syrup. Build up or dress the oranges in their compotier in an elevated pyramidal form; and the last thing before sending to table, pour the syrup all over the compote.

COMPOTE OF ORANGES À L'ESPAGNOLE.

Prepare some chestnut paste, and rub this through a coarse wire sieve into a compotier, moving the sieve round, so as to admit of the vermicellied paste falling in a conical heap in the centre of the compotier; set this in the screen in order to dry the vermicellied paste somewhat crisp.

When about to finish the compote, place neatly round the base a close border of compote of oranges, and pour some of the syrup all round the fruit.

Serve some iced whipped cream separately, to be eaten with this compote.

APRICOT COMPOTE.

Take well-grown apricots which are not entirely ripe, cut them in two, and peel them; rinse them in cold water, and blanch them, not too soft, in clarified sugar; let them stay in the sugar till they are cold, then put them to drain; add some apple-jelly to the sugar, and let it boil to a bead; put the apricots with the stone between into compote dishes, and pour over the sugar.

CHESTNUT COMPOTE.

Make a few slits in the chestnuts, roast them in the oven, or in an iron saucepan over a coal-fire, take off the shell, and press them flat; lay them in a saucepan, pour over clarified sugar, stand them in an oven, or let them heat by a gentle fire, but not boil; put them in compote dishes, cook the sugar to a thread, pour it over them, and add the juice of a sweet orange: these are Marrons, not American chestnuts.

CHESTNUT COMPOTE WITH CREAM.

Roast the nuts, press them flat, and put them in compote dishes; put the yolks of three eggs in a kettle, and stir in gradually a pint of sweet cream: cook to brittleness a quarter of a pound of sugar, with some dried orange-flowers; let it burn a little, that it may be yellowish, pour it into the cream, and, stirring constantly, let it boil up once; then strain it through a hair sieve on the chestnuts.

STRAWBERRY COMPOTE.

Take fine, not too ripe strawberries, wash them in cold water, and let them drain on a sieve; to one quart of strawberries, boil to a flake three-fourths of a pound of sugar, put in the berries, and let them all boil up gently once; care must be taken that they do not separate; skim them well, and put them in compote dishes.

Raspberry and currant compotes are prepared like the strawberry.

GREEN GOOSEBERRY COMPOTE.

Take fine, well-grown, unripe gooseberries, cut off the tuft, and make a slit in the side; take out the seeds, put the berries in water, and let them boil up once; cover them with a napkin, and let them stand till they are cold; put them again on the fire with the same water and let them heat, but not boil; put them in cold water, and, when they are cold, drain them; clarify and cook some sugar to a thread, let the berries boil eight minutes in it, skim them, and let them stand covered till the next day; then let them boil up several times with the sugar; skim them, and, when they are cold, put them in compote dishes; boil the sugar to a small bead, and pour it over.

CHERRY COMPOTE.

To one pound of stoned cherries, clarify and boil to a large flake five-eighths of a pound of sugar; put in the cherries, and let them boil up several times; drain them on the skimming-spoon, and put them in the dishes, and add to the juice a glass-full of currant-juice; let it boil to a weak jelly, and pour it half cold over the cherries.

PEACH COMPOTE.

Take well-grown, yet somewhat unripe peaches; cut them in two, and take out the stones; put them in boiling water, and let them stay there till they are soft, then throw them in cold water till cold; peel them, put them in refined sugar, let them boil up several times, drain on the skimming-spoon, and put them in compote dishes; add some apple jelly to the peaches, let it boil to a thin jelly, and pour it over the fruit.

ANOTHER PEAR COMPOTE.

Pare the fruit, and cut off the stems; if a good kind of pear, cut them in two, and put them in cold water, in which is the juice of a lemon; soften them in hot water, lay them in clarified sugar, and let them cook a quarter of an hour; take them out with the skimming-spoon, let them drain, and put them in compote dishes; add some apple jelly to the syrup, boil it to a small bead, and pour it over the fruit.

COMPOTE OF ROAST PEARS.

Take cooking pears, roast them till the skin is entirely burnt, put them in cold water, and take off the burnt skin; take white sugar, with a handful of dried orange-flowers, boil it up once, strain out the flowers, put in the pears, and boil the sugar to a bead; when they are cold, put them in compote dishes.

GRAPE COMPOTE.

Cut a slit in one side, take out the seeds, put the fruit in cold water, and let them boil; take them off the fire, let them stand covered some time, and put them in cold water; when they are entirely cold, take them out with a skimming-spoon; put them in clarified sugar boiled to a thread, and let them boil up some time, skim them, and, when they are cold, put them in compote dishes; boil the sugar to a small bead, and pour it over.

SALADE D'ORANGES.

Peel the oranges whole, removing the peel entirely down to the transparent pulp of the fruit; cut the oranges in slices, pick out the pips, and dish up the salad in a pyramidal heap; boil some syrup to the ball degree, add a glass of rum or brandy, give the whole a boil up, and, when cold, pour this over the compote. If preferred, some powdered sugar mixed with the brandy may be used instead of the syrup.

COMPOTE OF ORANGE BASKETS FILLED WITH FRUITS.

Select seven oranges of equal size; with a small sharp knife cut out two quarters from the upper part of the fruit, so as to leave a band measuring a quarter of an inch wide; this band will form the handle; pass the knife all round inside the band and level with the bottom pulp, and remove the piece of orange; with the edge of the bowl of a tea-spoon detach the remaining pulp and dexterously remove it, without tearing or in any way damaging the shape of the basket which will thus be formed; as the baskets are so far prepared, let them be dropped into a pan of cold water, and give them a simmer in boiling water on the fire for three minutes; this process will soften the peel, and enable you to stamp out the handle and edges with a tin perforating cutter, so as to represent open work; cut out such portions of the edges of the peel as will complete the scallops. When all the baskets are ornamented, give them a gentle simmer with twenty-four degrees syrup in a sugar boiler, and put them aside in a basin with their syrup till the next day. The syrup alone must be boiled up twice more, at intervals of several hours, and each time poured back on the orange baskets. When about to dish up the compotes, drain the baskets, fill them with a variety of small fruits of such kinds as are usually prepared for *macédoines;* these should be mixed with a little apple or orange jelly; pour over all some syrup flavored with maraschino.

NOTE.— Previously to cutting out the baskets, the oranges should be turned *very* thinly and spirally; this part of the process renders the fruit transparent.

COMPOTE OF LEMON BASKETS

Proceed as for orange baskets, using cadrati or citronelle liqueur to flavor the syrup.

COMPOTE OF CHERRIES.

Fine large cherries are best adapted for making compotes; cut the stalks to within half an inch from the fruit, and, when all are so prepared, drop the cherries into some syrup in a sugar boiler, give them a gentle simmer on the fire for three minutes, pour them carefully into a basin, and, when dishing up the compote, place the cherries in symmetrical order in the compotier, with their stalks upright, out of the syrup; add a little syrup flavored with noyeau.

COMPOTE OF CURRANTS.

Choose the finest fruit; pick the berries from the stalks carefully, without bruising or tearing them, and drop them into hot syrup of twenty-two degrees strength, give them a simmer without boiling, pour gently into a basin, and, when cold, dish them up in their compotier in the form of an elevated cone, and pour the syrup round the base.

NOTE. — Compotes of white and black currants are prepared as above.

COMPOTE OF CURRANTS IN BUNCHES.

Dip each bunch of currants, holding one end of the stalk, in tepid water, drain them on a sieve, and set them to dry for a few minutes in the screen or hot closet.

Whip the white of an egg with a wineglassful of water, and as soon as both are become froth, and incorporated, add a good dessert-spoonful of icing-sugar; mix and strain through a sieve into a basin.

Next, dip each bunch of currants in the egg-water, shake off any superfluous moisture, roll them thoroughly and lightly in some fine powdered sugar previously warmed in the screen for the purpose; and, as the bunches are thus sugared over with a semi-transparent coating of icing, place them neatly upon a wire drainer (see Adams's Illustrations), and put them for a few minutes to dry in the screen. When dishing up, arrange the currants in a pyramidal form upon vine-leaves in their compotier.

NOTE. — A number of pretty compotes may be thus prepared by using for the purpose any kind of small fruits, such as red, black, and white currants, cherries, strawberries, raspberries, plums, &c.; a variety of these, for sake of change, may form a single compote.

COMPOTE OF PLUMS.

Pick off the stalks, prick the plums all over with a pin, and let them simmer in syrup a little longer time than for cherries: in all other respects, this compote is prepared in the same way.

NOTE. — All compotes of plums are to be made in the same manner.

ANOTHER COMPÔTE OF APRICOTS.

Split the fruit in halves, peel them thinly and smoothly, let them simmer in thin syrup for a few minutes, add the kernels, and dish them up in a pyramidal form, with their syrup over the compote.

COMPOTE OF GREENGAGES.

Pick off the stalks, prick them all over, let them simmer in syrup, and serve as above.

For appearance' sake, the greengages may be colored green, as directed previously.

COMPOTE OF POMEGRANATES.

With the point of a small knife cut out a circle, the size of a five-shilling piece, off the peel of the pomegranates; then split down the sides of their skins, and carefully remove the bright ruby pips, without bruising them, into the compotier: pour some syrup flavored with orange-juice or maraschino over the compote.

COMPOTE OF ARLEQUINADE.

Prepare some pear-paste as directed for apple-paste, and proceed in the same manner.

COMPOTE OF GREEN FIGS.

The same as for greengages.

ANOTHER COMPOTE OF PEACHES.

Divide the peaches in halves, let them simmer in twenty-two degrees syrup for a few minutes to loosen their skins, remove these, and put the peaches back into the syrup with the addition of a gill of red-currant-juice, give the whole a gentle boil for a few minutes, remove the scum, and, when cold, dish up the compote with its syrup over it.

COMPOTE OF PEACHES GRILLÉS.

The same as compote of apples *grillés*.

ANOTHER COMPOTÉ OF PINE-APPLE.

Peel the fruit thoroughly; cut it up in slices; give them a few minutes' boiling in twenty-two degrees syrup; dish them up in the compotier, each slice overlapping the other; and pour some of their syrup over the compote.

COMPOTE OF WHOLE ORANGES.

Turn the oranges very thinly and spirally; score them all over in ornamental designs, formed by making transverse incisions, and cutting out the design in streaks, curves, rings, &c.; let them be first gently boiled in water for about twenty minutes, and afterwards simmered in syrup for other twenty minutes; allow the oranges to remain in their syrup for several hours: dish up the compote with their syrup poured over it the last thing before sending to table.

COMPOTE OF WHOLE LEMONS.

The same as oranges.

COMPOTE OF IMITATION GINGER.

Pumpkins, cucumbers, and salsifies may be advantageously used for the purpose. When pumpkins or cucumbers are used, they should be peeled, and cut into shapes in imitation of green ginger, and very gently simmered for a few minutes in syrup prepared as follows:—

To a pound of loaf sugar add a tablespoonful of savory and Moore's essence of Jamaica ginger, the juice of a lemon, and half a pint of water; boil up the syrup separately from the ginger three times, adding a little essence each time.

When salsifies are used for imitating ginger, they should be cut in different lengths and knotted shapes, peeled round the stalk instead of being scraped, parboiled in water with lemon-juice until half done, drained, and put into a sugar boiler with twenty-eight degrees syrup, two tablespoonfuls of

Compotes.

essence of ginger, and the juice of a lemon; simmer very gently for ten minutes, and boil up the syrup twice more.

COMPOTE OF CHESTNUTS GLACÉS.

Split the skins of the chestnuts across the rounded part, parboil them in water for five minutes, and roast them in the oven; when done, carefully remove their hulls, squeeze them rather flat with a napkin, and stick two together with some apricot jam. When all are so far prepared, hold each on a fork, and dip it in sugar boiled to the crack; and, as they are turned out of hand, place them on a wire drainer resting upon a baking-plate; dish up the compote in a pyramidal form, and pour some orange-flavored syrup round the base.

COMPOTE OF CHESTNUT PASTE.

Roast fifty chestnuts, clear them from all skin, and rub them while hot through a coarse wire sieve on to a dish. Boil twelve ounces of sugar to the ball degree, add the pulp of the chestnuts, work all together in the sugar-boiler with a wooden spoon on the fire, and, when well mixed, put the paste aside for use. Take small quantities of the paste in your hand, roll this into a ball, and shape it in the form of a chestnut; and, when all the paste is thus used up, place the chestnuts on a baking-plate to dry in the screen: they are then to be covered all over with apricot jam, rolled in powdered sugar, and dried on a wire drainer in the screen; after which they are to be dipped in sugar boiled to the crack, and dished up with syrup flavored with curaçoa round the base.

COMPOTE OF VERMACELLIED CHESTNUTS.

Prepare the paste as directed in the foregoing, let it be strongly flavored with vanilla sugar, and, while hot and just off the fire, rub it through a coarse wire sieve into the compotier in a raised pyramidal form; set it in the screen to be dried crisp, and with a teaspoon place small round heaps of whipped cream round the base.

COMPOTE OF GREEN WALNUTS.

Walnuts are said to be green when the kernels are just formed, and before the shells have become hard, though nearly ripe. The walnuts must be split through their natural division, and the point of a knife inserted and passed all round the inner part of the shell to extract the kernels; these must be divested of the white pith that surrounds them, and dropped into cold water acidulated with lemon-juice to keep them white.

Just before sending the compote to table, drain the walnuts dry, put them in a heap in their compotier, and add some syrup flavored with white noyeau.

COMPOTE OF GREEN FILBERTS.

Extract the kernels, skin them, soak them in acidulated water, and finish the same as walnuts.

COMPOTE OF BARBERRIES.

Pick the bright-red ripe barberries, wash them once in water, and drain them; let them simmer gently for ten minutes in syrup; and dish them in a compotier with their syrup.

COMPOTE OF AMERICAN CRAB-APPLES.

These are very small red apples resembling large cherries; leave the stalks on, let them simmer for ten minutes in syrup, dish them up with their stalks upright in their compotier, reduce their syrup, and pour it over the compote.

COMPOTE OF CRANBERRIES.

Drain them on a sieve, boil their juice with a few drops of cochineal, six ounces of sugar, and a little lemon-juice; serve the compote with its own syrup.

COMPOTE OF GRAPES.

All kinds of grapes suit this purpose; proceed as for currants.

COMPOTE OF DRIED NORMANDY PIPPINS.

Soak the pippins in tepid water for half an hour; throw this water away; let them simmer with a pint of cider and six ounces of sugar, with cinnamon and lemon-peel, for half an hour; dish up the pippins in their compotier; boil the syrup till it jellies, and pour it over the compote.

COMPOTE OF COCOANUT, WHITE.

Saw the shell of the cocoanut, and divide it in quarters, pell off the brown skin, and soak the clean pieces in cold water with lemon-juice and a little salt; first cut these in thin slices, and afterwards in thick thread-like shreds, resembling vegetables cut for julienne soup; as these are shred in small quantities out of hand, let them be dropped into a basin of cold water with lemon-juice and a little salt, and allow the shreds to soak in this for an hour. At the end of this time, the prepared shreds are to be drained on a clean sieve, washed in another water to free them entirely from the oil which exudes, and drained again on the sieve.

Boil one pound of the finest loaf-sugar to the blow, remove it from the fire, throw in the prepared cocoanut, give all a boil up on the fire, stirring lightly with a silver fork, and then lift out the shreds with the fork, well drained from the sugar, and place them on a sieve; boil up the sugar, throw in the cocoa, give it another boil on the fire, and drain it again; add a few drops of lemon-juice to the sugar, boil it to the pearl, throw in the cocoa, move it lightly, and lastly drain it on a sieve; separate the shreds carefully with two silver forks, one held in each hand, and, when cold, dish up the cocoa in an elevated pile in its compotier; pour round the base some clear syrup flavored with cedrati liqueur.

COMPOTE OF COCOANUT, PINK.

Proceed as in the foregoing, adding a few drops of prepared cochineal to give a pink tinge to the sugar.

COMPOTE OF DRIED FRUITS IN APPLE JELLY.

Have ready a variety of small dried fruits of different kinds and colors, such as American crab-apples, cherries, apricots, pine-apples, green apricots, pieces of apple, &c.; place some of these mixed in small coffee-cups or in jelly-glasses, fill up with bright apple jelly poured in hot, and, when thoroughly set and cold, turn them out, without breaking their shape, into their compotier.

COMPOTE OF SPANISH BRANCO.

Take the white part only of the breast of a roast fowl, free from fat and skin, chop, and then pound this in a mortar, adding half a gill of cream, and rub it through a fine wire sieve on to a plate. Mix eight ounces of the finest rice-flower in a sugar-boiler with the pulp of the fowl, six ounces of fine sifted sugar, a pinch of salt, and a gill of cream; stir this on the fire until it becomes a firm, compact kind of paste, and, when cold, divide it into small quantities of the size of a filbert, and roll these with your hands into the shape of sparrows' eggs; roll them in some *browned* Savoy biscuit-powder, place them symmetrically on a clean baking plate, and give them five minutes in a moderate heat. Dish up the compote in a square conical form, and pour some lemon or cinnamon flavored syrup round the base of the branco.

COMPOTE OF SANDWICHES À LA SEVILLANE.

Beat up twelve yolks of eggs with half a gill of cream and a dessert-spoonful of vanilla sugar, put some thin syrup about twenty degrees strength in a sautapan to boil on a stove,—

the syrup must rather simmer than boil, — use a dessert-spoon to drop carefully, and at once, a spoonful of the preparation in different parts of the syrup, thus forming small round pats; and, as these are poached on one side, turn them over with a fork, and, when done on both sides, drain them on a sieve or napkin: use up the whole of the preparation in this way. The poached pats of egg ready, stick two together with orange marmalade, stamp them out neatly with a circular tin cutter, and place them out of hand in close order upon a clean baking-sheet; shake some cinnamon sugar over their surface, give them a gloss with the red hot salamander (light color), dish them up spirally in their compotier, and pour round the base some syrup flavored with orange-juice and a little rum.

COMPOTE À LA XIMENES.

With some stale brioche, or any other similar kind of cake, cut out some small thin ovals about the size of a small egg, place these, with some thick syrup, in a sautapan to boil sharply on the fire, allowing the syrup to become caramelled, or, in other words, to attain a light-brown color; keep moving the pan about to prevent the *crusts* from sticking and becoming *burnt*, — they should be glossed with the sugar on *one* side at least, — and, as they are finished out of hand, place them, the brightest side uppermost, on a wire drainer in the cool.

To dish up this compote, a little Spanish branco should be strewn at the bottom of the compotier, and also a small heap (vermacellied through a wire sieve) in the centre; build the glossy crusts round the branco in three graduated tiers, using apricot jam to make them hold together in the desired position; fill up the centre with vermacellied branco, and strew cinnamon sugar over this, leaving the crusts perfectly glossy. Pour some orange-syrup round the base.

COMPOTE OF SPANISH VERMACELLI.

Break eight fresh eggs into a perforated flat tin strainer, dividing the yolks with the shell, and gently rub them through with the point of a spoon into a basin. Boil a pound of sugar to the feather degree ; pour the eggs into a small pointed tin funnel with a handle, stopping the hole with the end of your finger, holding the funnel in your right hand, and, as you commence letting out the egg from the point of the funnel, dropping it into the boiling syrup at the edge of the sautapan ; withdraw your finger from the hole, and direct the funnel all round the sautapan, in spiral rings, converging towards the centre ; let the funnel now be held by another person, and, as the egg becomes sufficiently set, take it out with a skimmer, and drain it on a sieve. Use up the remainder of the egg in this way ; and, when all is vermacellied and poached and drained, sprinkle some orange-flower water over them, and with two forks lift them lightly, in order that they may be thoroughly impregnated. Dish up the compote in a pyramidal heap, pour over all some light syrup, and ornament the base with rings of angelica.

PRUNE COMPOTE.

Soak one pound of prunes in water over night, drain them, put them in a saucepan with water, cover the saucepan, and let them boil over a moderate fire ; when they begin to soften, add a glass of red wine with four ounces of sugar, and let it boil till the prunes are cooked ; take them from the fire, rub a piece of sugar over an orange or lemon, and, when it is saturated with the zest, put it in the dish with the prunes : it is not indispensable to soak the prunes over night.

PINE-APPLE COMPOTE

Is made in several ways : one is, to peel the pine-apple, cut it in thin slices, and boil it up several times. The second

Compotes.

is, to place the slices in a dish, and sprinkle them with powdered sugar: this preparation serves two purposes; it can be used as a compote or salad; in the latter case pour over a little rum.

DIPLOMATIC APPLE COMPOTE.

Divide whole apples with a horizontal cut; remove the cores; boil them to a suitable degree; take them from the fire, and place them, with the flat side downwards, in the dish; pour on a fine marmalade of apricot until the pieces of apple be covered, and then pour over a syrup; cut in pieces a few shelled pistachios and preserved fruits that you strew over the compote. Pistachios and cherries make a very fine effect.

PORTUGUESE COMPOTE.

Cook the apples whole, as for diplomatic compote; put their peelings in a saucepan with a very little water, then take as many pippin apples, cut them in thin slices, and put them with the peelings on the fire; cook them until it is in marmalade; pour the marmalade upon a sieve standing over a dish; let it drain; add to the juice an equal weight of white sugar; let it boil up twice over the fire, and pour it on a round sheet of paper the size of the compote, turning up the edges to hold the jelly in, or else pour it on a plate rubbed with almond oil, and let it stand to cool. Decorate the whole apples standing in the dish with preserved fruits, such as cherries and others, and cover them with a sheet of jelly by turning the plate or paper upside down over them. In order to detach the jelly from the paper, moisten the latter with a sponge.

DIVERSIFIED COMPOTE.

This compote can be varied infinitely in the hands of a skilful workman. Cut apples or pears either in halves or quarters; put them in water acidulated with lemon-juice; cut them into the form of different fruits or vegetables, as apples, pears, apricots, carrots, mushrooms, &c.; cook them like the apple compote, and, ranging them on the compote dish, make use of rind of preserved oranges, &c., for leaves and foliage, and pour on the syrup.

THE END.

LIQUID RENNET,

FOR MAKING, IN A FEW MINUTES,

Delicious Desserts.

Yields, with milk, the most luscious of all desserts, the lightest and most grateful diet for invalids and children. Milk contains every element of the bodily constitution; when coagulated with Rennet, it is always light and easy of digestion, and supports the system with the least possible excitement. The convenience and nicety of this article, over the former troublesome and uncertain way of preparing Slip, Junket, and Frugolac, will recommend it at once to all who use it. There are few desserts so economical, delicious, and healthful.

This preparation, made of the clear, fresh Rennet of the calf, preserved with white wine, excels in purity of material, pleasant flavor, and every desirable quality.

LIQUID RENNET

Housekeepers will find in the Liquid Rennet a valuable acquisition: it is no trouble to use; and being economical, convenient, and healthful, a single trial is a certain recommendation. It is specially valuable in the summer season, as a diet for invalids and children, when suffering from or threatened with the complaints incident to change of water, too free indulgence of fruit, or deficient nutrition. Families with children seeking health in the country, where fresh milk is abundant, should be provided with a bottle of Rennet as an indispensable article.

As a food, milk is highly nutritious, and, when coagulated with Rennet, gives very mild, light, and easily-digested diets, devoid of stimulating properties. The addition of brandy, wine, spices, &c., increases the stimulant effect, and may be added when such effect is desired.

RECIPES FOR USING LIQUID RENNET.

SLIP — *Curds and Whey.* — Add two teaspoonfuls to a quart of milk slightly warmed: a firm curd will be produced in a few minutes. The addition of an egg to the milk, before adding the Rennet, gives an additional richness.

JUNKET — *Cold Custard.* — To a quart of milk warmed, add a tablespoonful each of sugar and brandy, and two teaspoonfuls of Rennet; stir only to mix, allow to cool, and flavor with nutmeg, as usual. More brandy and sugar may be added if desired.

FRUGOLAC. — This novel and very agreeable dessert may be prepared by adding the sirup that forms by the addition of sugar to strawberries, raspberries, sliced pine-apples, or other fruit, or two or three tablespoonfuls of fruit sirup or jelly to the surface of the junket or cold custard, after it has formed.

Prepared by

JOHN WYETH & BRO., Chemists,
1412 Walnut Street, Philadelphia.

SOLD BY ALL DRUGGISTS AND GROCERS.